The Apostles' Creed

"Not long ago the Apostles' Creed was known by heart by a great number of people. It is an ancient, succinct summary of Christian belief, expressing the great fundamentals of faith relating to God as Father, Son and Hoy Spirit. Alan Robinson's phrase-by-phrase commentary offers a comprehensive analysis, rich in bible references and application to the modern world. It will refresh those who have known and loved this statement of faith for many years, and will enlighten the newcomer equally.

May this book serve to renew the use of the Apostles' Creed in contemporary worship, in personal devotion and in studies which introduce the faith and apply it to daily life."

The Right Reverend Jonathan Bailey, Bishop of Derby

The Apostles' Creed
God's Special Revelation

ALAN ROBINSON

THE Alpha PRESS

BRIGHTON • PORTLAND

2 4 6 8 10 9 7 5 3 1

First published 2005 in Great Britain by
THE ALPHA PRESS
PO Box 2950
Brighton BN2 5SP

and in the United States of America by
THE ALPHA PRESS
920 NE 58th Ave   Suite 300
Portland, Oregon 97213–3786

The cover illustration shows a dossal made by Isabel Glover which hangs in
the Lady Chapel of St Peter and St Paul's Church, Swaffham.
Thanks are due to the Vicar of the church, Revd John Smith,
for permission to use the photograph, which is an
original taken by the author.

British Library Cataloguing in Publication Data
A CIP catalogue record for this book is available from the British Library.

Library of Congress Cataloging-in-Publication Data
Robinson, Alan.
The Apostles' Creed : God's special
    revelation / Alan Robinson.
    p. cm.
    ISBN 1-898595-46-1 (pbk. : alk. paper)
    1. Apostles' Creed—Study and teaching.
    I. Title.
BT993.3.R63 2005
238′.11—dc22

                                2004021208
                                CIP

Typeset and designed by G&G Editorial, Brighton
Printed by MPG Books, Bodmin, Cornwall
This book is printed on acid-free paper.

Contents

CONTENTS

Preface

The Apostles' Creed is "A statement of faith used only in the Western Church. Like other ancient Creeds, it falls into three sections, concerned with God, Jesus Christ, and the Holy Spirit, corresponding to the three baptismal questions of the primitive Church."[1]

This creed gives a brief summary of the Christian faith and is based on biblical authority, as may be observed in the biblical references used in this book. The Apostles' Creed has evolved into its present form from earlier creeds known to be in existence as early as the second century AD.[2]

Other important Christian creeds are the Nicaean Creed and the Athanasian Creed. These are much more complex than the Apostles' Creed, which is written in simple though precise language. A knowledge of the Apostles' Creed is essential for any true understanding of the Christian faith.

The Creed is explained and discussed by breaking the text down into twenty-two chapters. Questions for discussion are provided at the end of each chapter, and an Other Activities section is provided at end of the book.

[1] Quoted from *The Oxford Dictionary of the Christian Church*, ed. F. L. Cross and E. A. Livingstone, Oxford University Press, 1997, p. 89.
[2] For example, the Old Roman Creed. See *ibid.*

The Apostles' Creed

I believe in God, the **Father** Almighty,
    creator of heaven and earth;
    and in Jesus Christ his only **Son** our Lord,

Who was conceived by the Holy Spirit,
    born of the Virgin Mary,
    suffered under Pontius Pilate,
    was crucified, died and was buried.

He descended into hell;
    the third day he rose again from the dead;
    he ascended into heaven,
    and sits at the right hand of God the Father;
    he shall come to judge the living and the dead.

I believe in the **Holy Spirit**;
    the holy Catholic Church;
    the communion of saints;
    the forgiveness of sins;
    the resurrection of the body,
    and the life everlasting.

                          Amen.

The Apostles' Creed, and all biblical quotations in the text, are from the
New Revised Standard Version of the Bible.

I Believe in God

What is life about? That question has been asked since human beings first had the capacity to think. One famous philosopher, in trying to work out what he believed, started with what he asserted to be beyond doubt. He said to himself, "I think: therefore I am."[3] From this premise he tried to work out logically what he could believe. He came to the conclusion that God exists.

Looking round the world today, it is easy to see that people believe in all kinds of ideas about life. Some believe in astrology and try to organise their lives according to birth dates in relation to heavenly bodies. Some people believe simply in the survival of the fittest, an idea derived mainly from Charles Darwin. Some people believe only in human values and call themselves humanists. Some people conclude that life is there to be enjoyed and don't worry about whether or not there is a God. Some people base their lives on political ideals which may or may not have a religious basis. Some people believe in fate or destiny, but not necessarily in God.

Those who do not believe in God may call themselves atheists, a word which literally means "no God." In

---

[3] Co*gito ergo sum*, a phrase used by René Descartes (1596–1650).

accepting such a belief they imply that there is no possibility that God might exist. Others call themselves agnostics, claiming that they have no knowledge of God, though admitting to the possibility that God might exist. There are also many people who would like to believe in God, but feel they cannot do so because they cannot find any proof of his existence. It is thought-provoking to realise that when all the adherents of all the major world religions are taken into account, the number of people in the world who believe in God probably exceeds the number who don't.

Over history there are records of many and varied religions. Along with religious beliefs in general, there are other connected ideas. Some religions believe in an afterlife as, for example, in ancient Egypt. Some religions believe that God or gods influence human lives. The ancient Greeks, for example, believed in many gods and thought that these mythical beings took an interest in human affairs. Many religions put forward the idea that God or gods created the world.

The ancient Babylonians told stories about the creation of the world by their gods. Moral systems are often connected with religions, particularly the major religions. For example, Islam, Judaism and Buddhism all have strongly expressed moral precepts. Communication between gods and men is usually another religious factor. This communication may take the form of prayer or religious ceremonies or, from the divine side, signs and portents. The social lives of believers in a particular faith are often dictated by their beliefs. Often, the beliefs of a religion are ordered into doctrines which the adherents are expected to accept. Most important of all, perhaps, people claim to have special spiritual experiences which are central to the way they live their lives. The big question is, what is the searching individual to make of this patchwork of religious faiths?

Faced with such a wide choice of faiths, why choose Christianity? It could be argued that many people are Christians because of an accident of birth. If a child has Christian parents he may well be led in the same direction. Then again, in a country with a largely Christian tradition it is more likely that some one will have a serious encounter with the Christian faith, rather than with another faith. Of course, such cultural lines are less easy to draw nowadays because in many countries several major faiths flourish simultaneously and converts may be attracted to any one of these faiths.

In any case, even if a child has been brought up in a Christian family there may come a time when he or she questions the tenets of Christianity. A very basic question asked by many young people is, *Does God really exist?* To adapt Descartes' words quoted above, some one might make a very basic statement such as: *God exists: therefore I am.* To a firm believer this is stating the obvious. However, to a non-believer the statement would be a non-starter. Of course, many people have tried to prove beyond doubt that God does exist. This is not the place to explore these arguments, though the curious could, for example, find the name of Thomas Aquinas in an appropriate encyclopedia. A summary of this famous theologian's arguments would be given in most general encyclopedias and these are of great interest.[4] However, even Aquinas himself concluded that the arguments have their limits, though he claimed they did support his Christian faith.

---

[4] See, for example, *The Encyclopedia Britannica* either in a library or on computer disk.

It is still important to note that there is a vital difference between proof and conviction. Personal experience, together with the testimony of other people, are more convincing than any academic arguments. Many Christians, if asked "How do you know God exists?" might reply, "Because I know him. I meet him every day. I talk to him." But how does somebody move from doubt to inner certainty? There is only one way to make this leap of faith. *Try Christianity and see if it works for you. Try saying some prayers and see what happens in your life.*

At the same time, the use of reason does support faith. As well as experiencing God each day, it is good to explore what God is like according to the Christian revelation. The main Christian source for knowledge of God is the Bible. However, in addition to the word of God in the scriptures it is also possible to argue that God has revealed himself to people through natural revelation. This means that by studying the world in which one lives, anyone is able to use reason to show that God must exist, or at least there is a high probability that he exists.

The Apostles' Creed is God's special revelation, and has been carefully constructed from biblical texts. Some people would argue that it is just as much an inspired document as the scriptures themselves. But the creed is a summary and naturally much more is said about God in the Bible, than in the summary. So, apart from the biblical data that feeds into the creed, which will be discussed in subsequent chapters, what else does the Bible say about God?[5] It would not be difficult to make a long list of divine characteristics as outlined in the Bible. However, for the purposes of this

[5] The Nicene Creed and the Athanasian Creed are also regarded as central to Christian doctrine and they are fuller than the Apostles' Creed.

book it makes more sense to select a few aspects of God's revealed character.

The following attributes will be discussed briefly and related to daily life: God is loving, merciful, righteous, gracious and demanding.

God is loving

Most people, unless they have been very unfortunate, have had the experience of loving some one and of being loved. Experience of love in the broadest sense leads to happiness. By contrast, those who are filled with hatred are often very unhappy people. Think of the most wonderful experience of love between human beings that you know about, either from experience or observation. To live daily within such a loving relationship must be breathtaking. Unfortunately that is an ideal which is difficult, or even impossible, to live up to. With most people there are times when loving relationships break down. However, God's love is never failing. He is never going to let people down, if they turn to him in faith. Imagine, then, a love that is never going to break down, a love that is never going to end. That is some love! But God's love is even greater than can be imagined or thought. Yet the riches of his love are freely available to every human being.

The people who wrote and edited the Bible had wonderful experiences of God and it is not difficult to find texts which describe the love of God. In fact, there are so many such texts that it would be impossible to quote them all in a short book. However, three texts are given, just to remind us of the breadth and depth of the divine love. One of the best known texts is: *For God so loved the world that he gave his only Son, so that everyone who believes in him may not perish but may have eternal life* (John 3:16). This thought is at the heart of the Christian faith and will be discussed later. Contrary to popular belief, the Old Testament contains a number of references to God's love. The prophet Hosea, for example, wrote: *When Israel was a child I loved him, and out of Egypt I called my son* (Hosea 11:1). This text expresses the prophet's belief that God had chosen the nation of Israel because of his love, and that he had delivered them from slavery in Egypt to show his love in a practical way. Returning to the New Testament, Saint Paul shows that he believed firmly in a loving God. To the church at Thessalonica he wrote: *May the Lord direct your hearts to the love of God and to the steadfastness of Christ* (2 Thessalonians 3:5). This saying shows that we need God's help to find his love, that God so loves us that he seeks us out. Unfortunately we sometimes reject this invitation. However, if we accept the call to be loved by God, our daily lives may be transformed. Then, whatever happens to us we can never be separated from God's love (see Romans 8:35–39).

God is merciful

In human affairs we all realise that in some countries which are run by unscrupulous dictators there is little chance of mercy for any transgression against the powers that be, even if the action is unwitting or legal. The authorities in such countries, however, may break international laws or moral laws with impunity because they are a law unto themselves. On a smaller scale, most people when at school have met teachers with very different attitudes. Some appear through a child's eyes to be more merciful than others. It is probably true to say that those teachers who are merciful, though firm, are the most popular teachers. Furthermore, many people have met bullies, especially in their school days. Bullies are often merciless when tormenting people, but cry for mercy when they themselves are threatened. To some extent, the capacity to be merciful depends on the ability to put oneself in the other person's shoes. This needs imagination and experience of relationships in which transgressions and consequent friction have been dealt with in a loving and merciful way. On the other hand, if people hold tight to resentment, then they are not going to learn much about being merciful.

God's mercy, of course, is given upon certain conditions. According to one of Jesus' parables, a king let a servant off repaying a debt. However, when that servant refused to show similar mercy to a debtor, the employer reversed his earlier decision (see Matthew 18:23–35). In a similar way, if we are unmerciful to those in some way under our authority, then we are not in a fit state to receive God's mercy.

There are many biblical texts which explain the mercy of God. In his second letter to Corinth Paul writes: *Blessed be the God and Father of our Lord Jesus Christ, the Father of mercies and God of all consolation, who consoles us in all our affliction, so that we are able to console those who are in any affliction* . . . (2 Corinthians 1:3–4). The Blessed Virgin Mary says in her song of praise (Magnificat): *His mercy is for those who fear him from generation to generation* (Luke 1:50). This implies that if we do not have respect for God and his laws, we are more likely to receive a hard lesson from God, rather than unconditional mercy. The Old Testament is also rich in allusions to God's mercy. One of the psalmists writes: *Gracious is the Lord, and righteous; our God is merciful. The Lord protects the simple; when I was brought low he saved me* (Psalm 116:5–6). Here again there is a pointer to the nature of the divine mercy. It is more likely to be given to those of simple heart than to those who plan cunning schemes for their own advancement.

To live each day in the knowledge of the mercy of God is a great blessing. In some circumstances we may feel we are at a low ebb. We may feel that friends have turned against us. Or we may feel inadequate in the face of some challenge. We may feel guilty and in need of forgiveness. If we pray to our merciful God, he will find a way to help us, whatever our problem, provided we are honest and straightforward about it. Then of course there is the Lord's Prayer to sustain us, especially the phrase: *Forgive us our trespasses as we forgive those who trespass against us.*

God is righteous

We tend to be suspicious of people who claim to be righteous and sometimes classify them as self-righteous. However, the person who is truly righteous is not likely to go around boasting about it. Goodness is associated with righteousness, although goodness is a softer and more general word.

It might be helpful, before considering the righteousness of God, to attempt to define what is meant by righteousness in human terms. To simplify the answer, we could say that a righteous person does what is right. This means that he or she has some sort of moral standard and acts upon it. However, even the very conscientious person may fall short of perfection in this respect and, as a result, does something that he feels to be wrong. In Christian terms, the righteous man or woman would not only try to keep God's laws, but would strive also to cultivate other virtues. As Saint Paul puts it: . . . *the fruit of the Spirit is love, joy, peace, patience, kindness, generosity, faithfulness, gentleness and self control* (Galatians 5:22). Human righteousness, then, consists of many associated Christian ideals.

God's righteousness is, of course, the source of human righteousness, the significant difference being that God is perfect in every respect. To live in association with perfect righteousness, which Christians attempt to do, is very challenging. The standards set before us, as in the Sermon on the Mount (see Matthew 5–7), are awesome. This collection of Christ's teaching, of course, is meant for our inspiration and does not define the fullness of the righteousness of God. However, the highest righteousness that can be imagined may provide just a glimpse of this aspect of the divine character. The Bible has much to say about the righteousness of God. The Psalms, for example, are a wonderful source of theological knowledge. One psalmist writes: *For the Lord is righteous; he loves righteous deeds; the upright behold his face* (Psalm 11:7 and see also Pss. 119:137; 129:4; 145:17). Saint Paul was very conscience of the righteousness of God. He wrote to the church at Rome: *(God) himself is righteous and . . . he justifies (makes righteous) the one who has faith in Jesus* (Romans 3:26). This means that, though we know we have many failings, yet the righteous God will help us to become righteous also. This, of course, needs our cooperation. If we try to live our faith, God will respond.

God is gracious

At the human level a gracious person may, among other qualities, display generosity, especially to subordinates. This accomplishment implies that the gracious person has enough sensitivity to grant favours without being overbearing or boastful. Good manners go with graciousness and the person receiving the benefit of some gift is not left feeling he has been treated with any degree of contempt. The gracious giver and the recipient of grace should both feel comfortable with each other.

The grace of God, in a similar way, implies that God bestows his favour upon people. This grace is free and does not have to be paid for with meritorious actions. However, anyone receiving God's grace, in whatever form, would undoubtedly wish to deal graciously and lovingly with other people. To be "in a state of grace" means being in good relationship with God and our neighbours. It also means that a spiritual transformation is on-going. This sounds other worldly but, in fact, it implies that at the practical level the person concerned is trying honestly to grow into his true self, to be a better person.

It is sometimes claimed by critics that the idea of a God being gracious to people would result in favouritism and that this shows that God does not really exist. The idea of receiving God's grace, in such a view, would simply mean that somebody had been fortunate by chance. This is similar to the argument about whether or not God answers prayers. However, God's grace is freely available to everyone and those who do receive special insights are expected to shoulder responsibilities appropriate to their calling. The most outstanding example in the Bible, or indeed in world history, of some one receiving God's grace is told in the story of the Virgin Mary. She knew she had been chosen for a unique vocation, but yet her reaction shows her surprise that some one like herself should be so chosen. In the poem sometimes called the Magnificat she says: . . . *my spirit rejoices in God my Saviour, for he has looked with favour on the lowliness of his servant* (Luke 1:47–48). When the angel Gabriel introduced himself to Mary to announce the news he said: *Greetings, favoured one! The Lord is with you* (traditionally *Hail Mary full of grace*) (Luke 1:28). As we all know, Mary accepted the invitation to be the mother of the Lord because she knew it was God's word to her.

One of the psalmists writes a prayer for grace (favour) from God on behalf of the congregation: *Let the favour of the Lord be upon us, and prosper for us the work of our hands – O prosper the work of our hands!* (Psalm 90:17). The people have had a difficult time, as described earlier in the psalm, and the prayer is a hope for better times to come, through the grace of God. In the New Testament grace is seen as coming through Christ and there are numerous statements to that effect, the majority in the letters of Saint Paul. There is the famous prayer called the Grace: *The grace of our Lord Jesus Christ, the love of God, and the communion (fellowship) of the Holy Spirit be with all of you* (2 Corinthians 13:13). Paul also argues very strongly that it is God's grace in Christ which saves us: *For by grace you have been saved through faith, and this is not your own doing; it is the gift of God . . .* (Ephesians 2:8).

In more recent times the famous hymn *Amazing Grace* written by John Newton (1725–1807) gives wonderful expression to the saving power of God's grace:

Amazing grace – how sweet the sound –
that saved a wretch like me!
I once was lost, but now am found,
was blind, but now I see.[6]

To rely upon God's grace is a good way to live. This does not mean that we need make no effort in our daily lives, but it does mean that God will give us the strength we need to go through each day. As Saint Paul wrote: *My grace is sufficient for you* (2 Corinthians 12:9).

God is demanding

It's no good thinking that practising Christianity means loafing around in an earthly paradise. Yes, God's love is wonderful. Yes, God is always there beside us. But – and it is a big but – privilege brings responsibility. God expects us to follow Christ in trying to live up to the ideal of service to our neighbour, that is, to every one around us. In the global village where we now live, this may include people from any part of any of the five continents.

In order to answer God's call to use whatever talents or abilities we have, it is necessary to undergo a realistic self-assessment. In many spheres of life there are self-assessment forms to complete to help people make a judgement on where they are and what they can offer. However, unless somebody wishes to use a questionnaire, it is perhaps more useful to jot down our own ideas honestly and in the privacy of our own thoughts. Nobody else can do this for us. It's no

---

[6] Quoted from Hymn 31 in *Mission Praise*, Marshall Pickering 1990.

good saying I'm not much good at anything. Everybody has something to offer to Christ in everyday terms. OK, those who can preach or write hymns, or paint pictures, or play music, or organise charities, are fortunate to have the capacity to do these things. But *What about me?* is the crux of the matter. In what ways, large or small can I do the work of Christ?

When God calls, no excuses are acceptable. Jesus said, in response to those making excuses: *No one who puts a hand to the plough and looks back is fit for the kingdom of God* (Luke 9:62). To attempt to describe all possibilities that Christian vocation might involve would be impossible. However, in any one Christian congregation, Mr Jones might be called to some form of lay leadership; Mrs Robinson might be called to look after the church hall; Mr Atkinson might be called to repair anything mechanical that goes wrong; Miss Cuthbertson might be called to start a flower arranging group. Others might be called to clean the church, to read lessons during a service, to host a house group, to welcome new members to the congregation, to visit people in need of help, to be a treasurer, to teach in a children's class during a service – and so on.

Many characters in the Bible were called to do difficult things for God. Some, like Jeremiah, felt unworthy to become a prophet. However, despite his misgivings, the call was so strong that he had to continue his work (see Jeremiah 1:6–7; 20:9). Saint Paul's situation was different. As a young man he was an enemy of the Church, but God called him to abandon his training as a Pharisee and to become a Christian missionary (see Acts 9:1–22; 13:1–3). Peter, despite his best intentions, had deserted Jesus just before the crucifixion, but the risen Jesus challenged Peter to hold to his vocation (see John 21:15–19). Over the centuries many other people have answered God's call and these exemplars challenge us to follow in their footsteps, however humbly.

Questions for Discussion

○ *Is it possible that God has revealed himself in more than one faith, for example, in Islam and Christianity?*
○ *Many people find it difficult to believe in a loving God. How can they be helped to overcome their difficulties?*
○ *Is it realistic for ordinary people to try to become righteous (though not self righteous)?*

-⤺ CHAPTER TWO ⤻-

The Father Almighty

Except in unusual circumstances, everybody has experience of parenthood, either as a child, or as a parent. The experiences people have in these relationships seem to vary. However, really bad parents are very much in the minority. Most parents have their good points, in that they love their children, but neither they nor their children are perfect. Consequently, there are fault lines and sometimes the relationship between parent and child breaks down. On the whole, though, the family relationship holds throughout life, and affection remains despite any ups and downs.

Of course, the biological function of the parent is to bring children into being. This is universal throughout the animal world. But is there a point in the growth of the baby inside the mother, or at birth, when God endows the child with the mind and spirit that will inhabit the body? This is a difficult question to answer, and many people would claim that birth is a natural process without any divine intervention. Yet, if God is in control of all things, there must be a sense in which he is involved. Furthermore, if God created all things, as Christians believe, then there is a very real sense in which God has brought into being (parented) the human race. In this case, God is our Father in a very practical sense, as well as in the spiritual sense.

Christians believe that God is an eternal Trinity of Father, Son and Holy Spirit, as the creed states. This means that God has always been the Father to the Son within the Godhead and that human parenthood is patterned on an already existing divine parenthood. At the same time, the male element is incidental. In other words God's parenting is neither male nor female. However, God is revealed in the Bible as a Father, and it is customary to think of him in this way. Of course, the revelation took place within a patriarchal society, so the reporting of the revelation took place in a culture where the Father was seen as the head of the family or clan. So, to counteract this cultural bias, why not change the creed to read *the Parent Almighty?* There is no logical reason against this, but it seems easier to stay with the tradition. For the same reason, while it would be just as accurate to see God as Mother, as some biblical texts do, there seems to be little point in changing the long-standing creed (see Isaiah 49:15).

It must be difficult for someone who has had a bad father to imagine what a perfect heavenly Father might be like. The very name Father conjures up images and our experience of fatherhood in the earthly sense may well colour our picture of God. The whole idea of God's Fatherhood is not helped by an image of an old man with a beard. Medieval paintings might well be responsible for this inadequate imagery. The word *father* is only one image among a number which try to portray God. Others include, for example, *king* and *shepherd*.

It may help our understanding to identify some aspects of human fatherhood which will help us to understand the mystery of God's Fatherhood. To say that fatherhood should involve love for children is an obvious parallel. A loving Father God must love us infinitely. But love does not necessarily mean that children get all they want or can do whatever they like. A good father disciplines his children until they are of an age to make their own decisions. He will sometimes say *no* or *maybe* when a child asks for something. So it may be with God. We may pray for something, for example, the healing of a very sick grandmother. However, God may have other plans. It may be time for the grand-mother to move on to the next stage of life, or it may be that the discipline needed to survive her sickness is part of her training for the next life.

Fathers also give their children pleasant surprises some-times. God the Father may well do the same for us. Fathers are usually willing to listen to their children's troubles. God undoubtedly does the same. Sometimes fathers conclude that their children need a sharp lesson. Many people believe that God has given them some such hard lesson. Sometimes a father says, *Yes, I agree that what you want to do is good, but the time is not yet right.* God may say the same thing to someone who wishes, for example, to follow a particular kind of Christian vocation.

Sometimes children are estranged from their fathers and may leave the parental home. There is a good story in the Bible about a son who does just that. He asks for whatever money is due to him, and off he goes and spends it all. He finds himself in dire straits, and eventually decides to return home where his father gives him a princely welcome (see Luke:15:11–32). In a similar way, we may stray far from God, but if we return to him and express our sorrow, there is always a welcome for us.

Jesus, the Son of God, frequently referred to his Father in heaven. He taught his disciples, and us, to pray using the Our Father prayer. To show how close the relationship with God the Father can be, Jesus sometimes called God Abba, which in Aramaic means something approximating to Daddy (see for example Mark 14:36). Quite often, prayers are addressed to the Father, but end with words like *through Jesus Christ our Lord*, which acknowledges that Jesus acts as a gateway to lead us to the Father.

The idea of God as Father is very ancient. In a song attributed to Moses, we read: *Is not he (the Lord) your father, who created you, who made you and established you?* (Deuteronomy 32:6). Similarly, the prophet Malachi writes: *Have we not all one father? Has not one God created us?* (Malachi 2:10). The New Testament is even richer than the Old Testament with allusions to God the Father, especially in John's Gospel and in Saint Paul's letters. For example, in his Gospel, John writes, quoting Jesus: *This is indeed the will of my Father, that all who see the Son and believe in him may have eternal life; and I will raise them up on the last day* (John 6:40). This verse seems to summarise the gospel and richly opens out our Christian hope. To take another example, *For this reason I bow my knees before the Father, from whom every family in heaven and on earth takes its name* (Ephesians 3:14–15). Paul is saying how fervently he worships God and, in particular, he makes the point (mentioned above) that human fatherhood depends ultimately on the Fatherhood of God.

To take our attempt to picture God the Father a stage further, he is, as the creed states, Almighty. How can we imagine a being who is all powerful? Even compared with oceans, earthquakes and storms, human power is puny, though human beings have invented very powerful machines which are physically stronger than we are. Perhaps the most powerful human invention is the hydrogen bomb or one of its derivatives. Even more powerful in nature is the explosion of a star, and what sort of power does it take create a galaxy or to bring about the Big Bang which some scientists believe brought the universe into being. So what we have to try to imagine is a God who is more powerful than nature or human invention can portray, because ultimately all of these things are due to God's creative activity.

To be aware that such a God exists and to live daily in his presence is both awesome and comforting. If God wished to do so, he could wipe out our universe in the blink of an eye. However, he has revealed himself as a loving God, as a God who can enter our lives in way which is enriching and empowering.

Inevitably, when natural calamities happen and many people are killed or injured, we are puzzled as to why a loving God allows such events to come about, when he has the power to do anything he pleases. There has never been a satisfactory solution to this problem of why innocent people suffer in this way, though arguments have been put forward. The bottom line is that we only see part of the picture, whereas God sees and knows everything. However, it takes a lot of faith to continue to believe in God when we lose someone we love in a natural disaster. Yet, many people know deep within that the loved ones they have lost are in God's care. More difficult, perhaps, is living with someone who has been seriously injured in what seems almost to be an act of God. This is a great test for the injured person, and it may be that God does sometimes test people to the limit of their endurance. Again, the bottom line is that beyond the end of this life there is a fuller and happier life so, whatever unhappiness we experience, God will eventually bring justice and love to every living soul. The Christian God is an Almighty God and rules over both heaven and earth (concepts discussed in CHAPTER THREE).

"Almighty God" is a title often used in prayers today, but it is a very ancient title for God. Tradition has it that Abraham used this name for God. In Genesis 17:1 we read, God speaking to Abraham: *I am God Almighty; walk before me and be blameless.* This is a promise to us as well as to Abraham. The Hebrew word "blameless" could also be translated "made whole". God will put us together when we have been broken. Some very comforting words are written in the Book of Psalms. For example, one psalmist writes: *You who live in the shelter of the Most High, who abide in the shadow of the Almighty, will say to the Lord, My refuge and my fortress, my God in who I trust* (Psalm 91:1–2). The author of the Book of Revelation in the New Testament experienced many strange visions. In one of them he saw some angel-like creatures worshipping God and heard these words: *Holy, holy, holy, the Lord God the Almighty,*[7] *who was and is and is to come* (Revelation 4:8). The writer here is emphasising the awesome aspect of God's nature. These quotations show that that we have a paradox in our image of God. He is holy and Almighty, but he is also comforting and loving.

Questions for Discussion

○ *Which aspects of God's Fatherhood do you find most helpful?*
○ *Can you think of a special time in your life when you have found it supportive to think of God as Father?*
○ *What mistakes do people make in their use of power over others? How is God's use of his power different?*

[7] The Greek word used here is *pantakratōr*, a title often used to refer to Christ.

CHAPTER THREE

*C*reator of Heaven and Earth

The Bible tells us that there was a beginning when God made heaven and earth (Genesis 1:1). Because our view of our world is different from that of the author of Genesis, this needs to be interpreted as meaning the universe – all that exists in the physical sense. Scientists have been arguing for some hundreds of years about how our universe began. One of the current theories postulates a huge explosion or a "Big Bang". If this did happen, then those who believe in God may suppose that a Big Bang was the way God started off the universe, that God was the cause of the beginning. Non-believers, on the other hand, have to solve the problem of what caused the Big Bang.

Living with an awareness of the Creator God can be an exciting experience. Christians believe that God takes an interest in his creation and, in particular, in every single person who comes into being. Not only does God take an interest in our created world, he also holds it in being and keeps creating and recreating it. This may be called the process of continuing creation. God does make things happen, but only in a way that does not remove our responsibility for our own lives and our environment. He may call people and guide them to act in certain ways. He may watch us grow, much as a gardener watches his flowers grow, and at times he may, like the gardener, give us an input or an impetus, or cut away old growth or diseased branches. This implies that our characters should develop over our life time. Experience teaches us much. It changes us. Perhaps what we have learnt is all we can take with us into the next life. If we have completely wasted our lives, then we can take very little with us. We certainly can't take possessions, honours or earthly glory. We should each of us, from time to time, ask the question: *What sort of person am I becoming?* That, after all, is what life is about. Further, we should consider whether we are cooperating with our Creator in working out our blueprint for the next stage of our existence.

In the broader sense also, we need to ask about the purpose of creation. It could be that this world is a training ground for the next life and that there is no long term aim for our world. However, there are several signposts in the Bible which seem to indicate that God has an ultimate end in mind for this world which amounts, in fact, to a new creation. For example, the prophet Isaiah describes an ideal world of the future ruled by a divinely chosen king. In this ideal world, *The wolf shall live with the lamb, the leopard shall lie down with the kid, the calf and the lion and the fatling together, and a little child shall lead them.* And also, *They will not hurt or destroy on all my holy mountain; for the earth will be full of the knowledge of the Lord as the waters cover the sea* (Isaiah 11:6, 9). The author of the Book of Revelation also has a vision of an ideal future for the world: *And I saw the holy city, the new Jerusalem, coming down out of heaven from God, prepared as a bride adorned for her husband. . . . I saw no temple in the city, for its temple is the Lord God the Almighty and the Lamb. And the city has no sun or moon to shine on it, for the glory of God is its light, and its lamp is the Lamb. The nations will walk by its light, and the kings of the earth will bring their glory into it* (Revelation 21:2, 22–24).

Passages like these are associated with Christian teaching about the Last Things,[8] which includes the belief that God's work in creation and history will have a final consummation. This doctrine will be discussed below in relation to the credal statement that Christ will come again.

One of the joys of living, given good health and a reasonable standard of life, is to admire the beauty and interest of the created world. It is a pity that we become so accustomed to our environment that we sometimes virtually ignore it because we are so busy. However, there are times when we do notice the beauty of a sunset, or of a primrose, or of a young foal or of a tree in spring. Yet again sometimes nature forces itself upon our attention in the form of a tornado or a volcanic eruption. Then we can see the power and majesty of the natural world. The teeming life on our planet and the pulse of growth in oceans, in forests or on prairies are fascinating. Fortunately, we can observe much of the spell-binding detail of nature's ways in TV programmes, which is good for us to do when so many of us live our lives in cities. It is difficult to imagine that there might not be a God who is the power behind our wonderfully complicated and interesting universe. Is it possible that all the beauty of nature, including our capacity to appreciate it, came about as a cosmic accident? Surely that does not add up.

One of the interesting facets of the biblical creation story is that the author of Genesis maintains that people are made in the image of God: *Then God said, "Let us make humankind in our image, according to our likeness; and let them have dominion over . . . all the wild animals of the earth . . . "*

[8] Eschatology.

(Genesis 1:26). There are various ways of interpreting this statement, but parts of our experience seem to imitate the divine experience in the sense that we have the capacity to think, to imagine and to create. It is a pity that many people do not develop their creative capacity. This is sometimes through lack of opportunity, or sometimes through diffidence. Everybody has some creative ability and once it is discovered it can be developed. If an educational system fails to help people to find their creative gifts, then that is a considerable shortcoming in that system. Of course, as well as enjoying the use of our own creative gifts, we can enjoy what other people create, for example, in art, music and literature.

The poets and prophets of the Bible had quite a lot to say about God and creation. This is mainly in the Old Testament because the New Testament writers were concerned with other matters, though they were obviously familiar with their scriptures (i.e. the Old Testament). Some of the psalmists praised God for the wonders of his creation. Take, for example, Psalm 104 in which the author writes: *O Lord, how manifold are your works! In wisdom you have made them all; the earth is full of your creatures* (Psalm 104:24). This psalm contains some beautiful poetic descriptions of the beauty and bounty of nature.

The prophet Amos, whose main message is about God's judgement, nevertheless expresses his admiration of God's creation: *The one who made the Pleiades and Orion, and turns deep darkness into morning, and darkens the day into night, who calls for the waters of the sea, and pours them out on the surface of the earth, the Lord is his name . . .* (Amos 5:8).

Even Job, who had dismal experiences, speculates about the source of wisdom: *God understands the way to it, and he knows its place. For he looks to the ends of the earth, and sees everything under the heavens. When he gave to the wind its weight, and apportioned out the waters by measure; when he made a decree for the rain, and a way for the thunderbolt; then he saw it and declared it; he established it, and searched it out* (Job 28:23–27).

Some biblical writers maintain that Wisdom, personified as a woman, was present at God's creation of the world. The author of the Book of Proverbs writes: *The Lord created me (wisdom) at the beginning of his work . . . .then I was beside him like a master worker; and I was daily his delight, rejoicing before him always, rejoicing in his inhabited world and delighting in the human race* (see Proverbs 8:22–31).

God the Father is usually taken to be the Creator, but God the Holy Spirit and God the Son were, of course, and still are, part of the divine creative process. The author of Genesis describes the situation at the beginning of creation: *. . . the earth was without form and void and darkness covered the face of the deep, while a wind (spirit)*[9] *from God swept over the face of the waters* (Genesis 1:2). John's Gospel famously makes it clear that the Son, the divine Word, was also present at Creation: *In the beginning was the Word, and the Word was with God, and the Word was God. He was in the beginning with God. All things came into being through him, and without him not one thing came into being* (John 1:1–3). This thought helps us to understand that the Incarnation was a second main stage in God's continuous creative activity.

The early chapters of Genesis tell the story of creation in poetic form. Whether or not different authors had a part in the writing is not as important as some scholars make out.

---

[9] The Hebrew word *ruach* means both spirit and wind. Some interpreters prefer to translate as "spirit".

The final version, though possibly edited from earlier versions, is what we have – and it is a very beautiful account of how God brought the universe in to being. The main point of this creation hymn (Genesis 1:1–2:4a) is that God spoke the word and creation happened. Out of a meaningless chaos he made our world and all the wonderful creatures and plants around us, as well as ourselves. The seven-day programme is incidental to this main point and may be interpreted in different ways.

The description of the first man (Adam) in a beautiful and fertile garden, together with his wife Eve, is intended to explain the frailties of human nature Genesis 2:4b-3:24). The writer is making the point that all people are sinful, which is true to our own experience. The poetic details of the story have their value, but they are incidental to the main theme of the Fall of Man. When it is considered that one of the main aspects of Jesus' work in the Incarnation was to bring about the transformation of man (potentially all of us), then the introduction to the story of humankind was set out in Genesis, developed over many centuries, and culminated in the Cross – the Cross being the second hinge of human development.

Saint Paul was fully aware of the flawed development of God's people and the grand culmination in the work of Christ in reconciling man to God. As well as commenting on the beginning of creation, and the Fall of man, he explains the Incarnation as God's way of capping the creation process in man. Of God's overall power in creation he writes: *Ever since the creation of the world his eternal power and divine nature, invisible though they are, have been understood and seen through the things he has made* (Romans 1:20). Of the new life in Christ he writes: *You were taught to put away your former way of life, your old self, corrupt and deluded*

*by its lusts, and to be renewed in the spirit of your minds, and
to clothe yourselves with the new self, created according to the
likeness of God in true righteousness and holiness* (Ephesians
4:22–24).

Worship of God as Creator should include thanksgiving
for our bodies, our minds, our five senses, our emotions and
our imaginations. Through these gifts we are able to appreciate the marvellous environment God has made for us.
Furthermore, these aspects of our personalities make up the
fertile soil in which the eternal parts of our being grow.
Often enough we talk about the soul or spirit as that part of
us which returns to God after we leave this life. It always
seems a pity when this aspect of our being is starved of the
sustenance it needs to develop. Our relationship with God
the Creator, among many other facets of our lives, is what
makes our sense of eternity tick.

Questions for Discussion

○ *In what ways can people help to look after the natural world?*
○ *Is an ideal world possible in this life?*
○ *Is beauty within us (in the eye) or outside us?*

CHAPTER FOUR

Jesus Christ

What would it have been like to be with Jesus, perhaps as one of his fringe disciples, as he wandered around Galilee and Judaea two thousand years ago. His friends and disciples would be people like ourselves. Even Jesus, at first glance, may have appeared ordinary, one of the crowd. Yet, a closer look, or experience of his teaching or healing, would surely have revealed in his personality something beyond the ordinary. Today we talk about people with magnetism or with charisma and, to be sure, some people we meet do seem to possess some special quality which distinguishes them from the crowd. However, compared with even the most gifted people we have ever met, the charisma of Jesus must have been extra-special. Yet, even the most important people among us, for example monarchs and politicians, cannot escape the passage of time and the passing from this life to what lies beyond. This was true of Jesus. As a human being it was his destiny to die, but he might, of course, have died in his bed. However, he died an ignominious death as a criminal, even though he was believed by some to be the Messiah. This manifest and complete humanity of Jesus is vital to any understanding of God's purposes in the Incarnation.

Jesus was not normally addressed as Christ (Messiah) during his life time on earth. Probably he would be known as Jesus, son of Joseph. Yet the name Jesus was a special one and, according to the birth stories in the New Testament, this name was chosen by an angel and told to Mary and Joseph. The name Jesus is special because in the Hebrew/Aramaic original it means Saviour. This means that Jesus may have been called Joshua, or a similar form, by his contemporaries (for example *yēšûa'*). The name Joshua comes from two Hebrew words meaning *God saves*. It is remarkable that millions of people over history have felt the saving power of Jesus, the one who at birth was given the name *Saviour*. This amazing and indisputable fact surely authenticates the Annunciation to Mary and Joseph.

The full name *Jesus Christ* was given to Jesus by his followers after his death and resurrection. The New Testament writers, of course, take the name for granted. In his introduction to his Gospel Mark writes: *The beginning of the good news of Jesus Christ, the Son of God* (Mark 1:1). The word Christ is from the Greek *Christos* which is a translation for the Hebrew word Messiah (mašiach). This word means *the one anointed* and when Israelite kings were installed, oil was used to anoint them. Take, for example, the account of Solomon's inauguration as king: *There the priest Zadok took the horn of oil from the tent and anointed Solomon* (1 Kings 1:39). Jesus knew that he was the anointed One, and when he read the lesson in the synagogue at Nazareth he said: *The Spirit of the Lord is upon me, because he has anointed me to bring good news to the poor . . .* Jesus' own comment on the reading was: *Today the scripture has been fulfilled in your hearing* (see Luke 4:16–21). The word used here for *anointed* is a verbal form from the same root as Christ. Of course, Jesus changed the whole concept of Messiah-ship into one of service, rather than one of kingly power, though to be sure he does have kingly power.

It can be seen, then, that the two parts of Jesus' name may be expressed as: *The King who saves (people).* This is a wonderful title and a perfect description of what Jesus Christ does for us. How do we live with this idea? Well, it is claimed by many people that Jesus saves them from danger, that he saves them from illness and hurt, that he saves them from temptation, that he saves them when they are lost. However, perhaps the most important aspect of Jesus' power to save lies in the idea that he saves us, all that we are in spirit, to live eternally with him. This process begins in the here and now, but continues throughout our lives. Yes, people do have special experiences of being saved, but that is only the beginning of their growth. Our spiritual preparation for the next life is progressive. It is more correct to say *I am being saved* than *I have been saved.* As Saint Paul wrote: *For the message about the cross is foolishness to those who are perishing, but to us who are being saved it is the power of God* (1 Corinthians 1:18). At the same time, those who insist on using the fulfilled form may be right in the prophetic sense that their conviction leads them to believe that they will certainly be saved eventually.

Jesus himself uses various metaphors to define his relationship with us. For example, he is the good Shepherd, he is the bread of life, he is the light of the world. Obviously there are numerous other functions of Christ which are extensions of his work as the *King who saves*, but only these three aspects of Christ's role will be discussed here.

As the good Shepherd *he lays down his life for the sheep,* unlike the hired hand who *runs away because a hired hand does not care for the sheep* (see John 10). The parable of the lost sheep, told by Jesus, emphasises the idea of the

Shepherd's saving function. He goes searching for the one that is lost, leaving the other ninety-nine until his search is successful (see Luke 15:1–7). It is important to note that the lost sheep is compared with a repentant sinner. This means that if we wander away from God and become selfish and uncaring, he will search us out and save us. However, our cooperation is an important factor in the situation. We will not be found unless we repent – turn away – from sin. The Shepherd is the *King who saves.*

As the bread of life sent from heaven, Jesus ensures our spiritual sustenance: *I am the bread of life. Whoever comes to me will never be hungry, and whoever believes in me will never be thirsty* (John 6:35). Of course, in the Lord's Prayer we do pray for our daily bread, but at this point Jesus is speaking about something else. At one level he is saying, *If you turn to me I can help you and your hunger and thirst for love and spiritual fulfilment will be satisfied.* At another level he is prophesying that his body will become the bread of life, as made clear at the Last Supper. *While they were eating, he took a loaf of bread, and after blessing it he broke it, and gave it to them, and said, "Take; this is my body"* (Mark 14:22). The body of Christ, sacrificed on the cross, continues through the sacrament of holy communion to sustain Christians all over the world. Each time we receive this bread of life, along with the wine, we are renewed and strengthened in body, mind and spirit. Yet again we are in relationship with the *king who saves.*

As the light of the world, Jesus Christ shows us the way, draws us towards the light of heaven. We all know what it is like to walk along a narrow path on a dark and stormy night. In such circumstances a light going before us can be very useful. Our lives can sometimes be dark and stormy and the way ahead may seem uncertain If, however, we follow the light of Christ, we shall find our way. The idea of a spiritual guiding light was not new to people of Jesus' time. Many would be familiar with the psalm which says: *Your word is a lamp to my feet and a light to my path* (Psalm 119:105). This is a helpful text, but the idea of Christ carrying that light before us makes the idea more personal. The famous picture of Christ carrying a lantern, painted by Holman Hunt, illustrates the point very well. However, Jesus' own words best summarise his promise to those who trust in him: *I am the light of the world. Whoever follows me will never walk in darkness but will have the light of life* (John 8:12). This is God's covenant with us through the *King who saves.*

Questions for Discussion

- *Was the crucifixion really necessary or could God have shown his love for us in some other way?*
- *In what ways does Jesus save?*
- *Will every human being without exception be saved ultimately in the spiritual sense?*

CHAPTER FIVE

God's Only Son

It seems a bit odd to describe somebody as the *only* Son of God. Why not simply Son of God? This description may have something to do with the fact that emperors at the time the Gospels were written claimed to be divine. To say, then, that Jesus was the only Son of God is to emphasise his uniqueness and to deny that any other human being could be a divine Son in the same way.

There are several mentions in the Gospels of people who have an only son or daughter, using the same word as applied to Jesus (see Luke 7:12; 8:42; 9:38). Apart from Jesus himself, there is at least one special case of an only son in the New Testament which is the reference to Isaac in the Old Testament who is described as Abraham's only son (see Genesis 22:2 and Hebrews 11:17). Abraham's intention to offer Isaac as a sacrifice at God's command, is sometimes taken as a pattern for God's sacrifice of his Son. However, an importance difference between Isaac's sonship and Christ's is that Christ *is* God. In other words, when Christ came to earth as a human being, it was God offering himself as a sacrifice. This, of course, is related to the idea that God is a Trinity of Father, Son and Holy Spirit.

While there are many references to Christ as God's Son in the New Testament, it is in John's Gospel and in one of

John's letters that we find references to Christ as the *only* Son of God. In the very first chapter of John's Gospel, the author makes it plain who Jesus truly is: *And the Word became flesh and dwelt among us, and we have seen his glory, the glory as of a father's only son* (John 1:14). More pointedly, perhaps, John writes: *No one has ever seen God. It is God the only Son, who is close to the Father's heart, who has made him known* (John 1:18).

Later in his Gospel, John writes: *For God so loved the world that he gave his only Son, so that everyone who believes in him may not perish but may have eternal life* (John 3:16 and cf. 3:18). This saying testifies that God the Son came to earth for our benefit. Those who have faith in Christ are promised eternal life. This is a wonderful prospect, but what of those who have not heard the gospel? No doubt they will receive God's grace in a different way. However, those who have heard the gospel and have rejected it, in effect have rejected Christ and God's love. So what happens to them? Perhaps they receive further opportunities in this life or the next to come to Christ. At the same time, God has given us freedom to choose and it is possible that someone might reject Christ permanently. Over against that idea, it may be asked whether God's love is ultimately resistible. Only God knows the answer to these questions.

It is clear from the scriptures that Christ came from God and returned to God after the Incarnation. In John's Gospel we read: *Jesus, knowing that the Father had given all things into his hands, and that he had come from God and was going to God, got up from the table, took off his outer robe, and tied a towel round himself* (John 13:3). This, of course, is preparatory to the washing of the disciples feet. Such a service from God himself to ordinary people like ourselves, is truly amazing. This is similar to the description of Christ given by Saint Paul in his letter to Philippi: *Let the same mind be in you that was in Christ Jesus, who, though he was in the form of God, did not regard equality with God as something to be exploited, but emptied himself, taking the form of a slave, being born in human likeness* (Philippians 2:5–7). God's Son, then, though of divine origin, and though destined to return to God, showed us a pattern for our behaviour in the way he lived and died. Of course, in his humanity he did not leave behind his Sonship of God. What he left behind deliberately was the glory of his divinity, so that we could see God's nature portrayed in a form we could readily understand. It is mysterious that a human being could at the same time be human and at one with the Godhead, but all existence is within God anyhow, so in a way God's Son simply moved from one part of the divine experience to another.

The main aim of the New Testament is to demonstrate that Jesus Christ was and is the Son of God. There are several passages which make this abundantly clear by describing special signs from God. For example at the baptism of Jesus a voice from heaven was heard saying, *You are my Son, and the Beloved; with you I am well pleased* (Mark 1:11). It is not clear from the wording if it was only Jesus who heard the voice, or whether the people present heard it. In either case, the evangelist is emphasising the divine Sonship of Jesus. At the Transfiguration also there was a heavenly voice. The three disciples present (Peter, James and John), after witnessing the strange transformation of Jesus on the mountain, heard a voice say: *This is my Son, the Beloved; listen to him* (Mark 9:7). A further example of a proclamation of Jesus' Sonship occurs in the story of Jesus walking on the water. On this occasion it was the disciples who made the statement after witnessing the miracle: *And those in the boat worshipped him, saying, Truly you are the Son of God* (Matthew 14:33). It is obvious that selected people of the time of Jesus were firmly convinced that he was God's Son. For those who question the signs, especially the heavenly voices, there are a number of other occasions when people are described as having auditions rather than visions, though sometimes the two are combined. A good example of an audition is the voice that came to Saint Paul when he was struck down on the Damascus road: *The men who were travelling with him stood speechless because they heard the voice but saw no one* (Acts 9:7). After such an experience it is not surprising that Paul was convinced that Jesus was the Son of God. In his letter to Rome he wrote: *I Paul, a servant of Jesus Christ . . . who was descended from David according to the flesh and was declared to be Son of God with power according to the spirit of holiness by resurrection from the dead . . .* (Romans 1:1 and 4).

The resurrection of Jesus must have convinced many doubters, including Thomas, that Jesus was God's Son. However, a Roman soldier who was presumably a Gentile, witnessed the crucifixion, and his reaction to this event was to say, *Truly this man was God's Son* (Mark 15:39).[10] The soldier was an unimpeachable eye-witness. As we say, he had no axe to grind. He must have seen many criminals executed. Yet, he saw in Jesus' suffering something so special that he believed Jesus to be divine. We can only speculate as to what it was that convinced the soldier. It may possibly have been the love that Jesus showed even in his painful dying.

The wonderful thing for us in believing that Jesus Christ is God's Son, is that we are drawn into what is essentially a

---

[10] Or *a son of God*.

family relationship. We, too, become children of God, brothers and sisters of Christ. Most of us, if we have been fortunate, have had experience of family love, but the love of God for us is much closer than anything we have ever experienced before. This is not a sentimental, wishy washy love. It is never failing, it takes risks, it is strong and rock-like. It includes compassion and forgiveness, but it also involves measured judgement. We sometimes need to learn hard lessons. However, when all the chips are down, God is our Father, Christ is our brother and the Holy Spirit is our companion. This is a family that never breaks up.

Questions for Discussion

○ *What is meant by eternal life in John 3:16?*
○ *Why did Jesus not reveal himself as a glorious Son of God during his earthly life?*
○ *How do you think Jesus became aware he was the Son of God as he grew up?*

CHAPTER SIX

Our Lord

The use of the word "lord" in the Bible is complicated. In both Testaments the Hebrew or Greek words respectively are sometimes used simply as a respectful form of address, much as people today might call some one "sir". Jesus is sometimes addressed as lord in this ordinary sense. For example, the foreign woman who asked Jesus to cast out a demon from her daughter said, *Sir (Lord), even the dogs under the table eat the children's crumbs* (Mark 7:28). Similarly, a royal official who was asking help for his sick son said to Jesus, *Sir, come down before my little boy dies* (John 4:49).

The experience of Mary Magdalene outside the tomb of Jesus after he had risen shows a fascinating use of the title. First of all, on seeing a person she thought was the gardener, she said, *Sir, if you have carried him (Jesus) away, tell me where you have laid him, and I will take him away* (John 20:15). Of course, she discovered she was actually speaking to Jesus, and when she went to tell the disciples, she said, *I have seen the Lord* (John 20:18). The same Greek word *(kurios)* is used in either case and it is likely that the evangelist is deliberately using dramatic irony. Mary unwittingly called Jesus lord or sir in the ordinary sense, but when she realised she had seen the risen Jesus, she called him Lord in the divine sense.

In the Old Testament, there is a similar ambiguous use of the Hebrew word for Lord. For example, the messenger who brought the news of Saul's death to David, calls David "lord" (2 Samuel 1:10). On the other hand, the writer of Genesis refers to God as the Lord Yahweh (usually translated as *Lord God*) (Genesis 15: 2,8). The four Hebrew letters which give God's name as Yahweh are YHWH.[11] In English translations this name is usually written as LORD. This tradition of translation arises from the practice of Jewish rabbis who were reluctant to pronounce God's name. When they were reading the scriptures they said the word LORD instead of Yahweh. This may well have been the case in the time of Jesus. In any case, "Lord" was a recognised title for God in Judaism and also for gods or spirits in other religions. One interesting example of this use lies in the name Adonis, which is virtually the same as the Hebrew *'ādôn (Lord)*.)

It is clear that the New Testament writers were convinced that Jesus was Lord in the divine sense. For example, Thomas is reported as saying to the risen Jesus, *My Lord and my God!* (John 20:28). Saint Paul frequently refers to Jesus as *Our Lord*. For example, he writes, *Am I not an apostle? Have I not seen Jesus our Lord?* (1 Corinthians 9:1). In the same letter Paul uses the phrase *Jesus is Lord* (1 Corinthians 12:3). This is generally accepted as the earliest confession of the Church and such a view is supported by Paul's comment in his letter to the Romans: . . . *if you confess with your lips that Jesus is Lord and believe in your heart that God raised him from the dead, you will be saved* (Romans 10:9). Paul further claims *that at the name of Jesus every knee should bend, in heaven and on earth and under the earth, and*

---

[11] An alternative interpretation translates YHWH as Jehovah.

every tongue should confess that Jesus Christ is Lord, to the glory of God the Father (Philippians 2:10–11).

Other implications of the Lordship of Jesus include the idea that he is Lord over all earthly rulers. Paul writes to Timothy: . . . *our Lord Jesus Christ . . . who is the blessed and only sovereign, the King of kings and Lord of lords* (1 Timothy 6:14–15 and see Revelation 17:14). Not only is Christ Lord over earthly powers, he is also Lord over life and death. Paul writes: *For to this end Christ died and lived again, so that he might be Lord of both dead and living* (Romans 14:9).

Even before Paul was converted, Peter preached a sermon on the Day of Pentecost in which he said: *Therefore let the entire house of Israel know with certainty that God has made him both Lord and Messiah, this Jesus whom you crucified* (Acts 2:36). There is a note of absolute confidence in this statement which is difficult to discount. In a later sermon to a group of Gentiles, Peter acknowledges that all nations are subject to Christ and have the right to come to him: *I truly understand that God shows no partiality, but in every nation anyone who fears him and does what is right is acceptable to him. You know the message he sent to the people of Israel, preaching peace by Jesus Christ – he is Lord of all* (Acts 10:34–36).

So what is it like to have the Lord of all as a daily companion? The close disciples of Jesus, of course, were with him constantly for about three years. They didn't realise at first that Jesus was their Lord in the divine sense, and perhaps it was not until after the resurrection that they fully understood this. Mark's Gospel in particular portrays the disciples as lacking such understanding. However, there was an important turning point in Jesus' ministry at Caesarea Philippi when Peter declared Jesus to be the Messiah. This is fully described in Matthew's Gospel and

Peter's words are: *You are the Messiah the Son of the living God* (Matthew 16:15). The Transfiguration of Jesus happened around the same time. From then on, Jesus was more open with his disciples and foretold his own death and resurrection several times (see Mark 9:30–32; Mark 10:32–34).

We can imagine, then, that when the disciples first started going around with Jesus, they probably thought he was a gifted and rather unusual teacher or rabbi. Gradually, as they observed his miracles and heard his remarkable pronouncements they would have begun to realise that he was very special. Then finally they understood, even if only partially, that Jesus was their Lord, and not simply their teacher. At the same time, during their years with Jesus they observed him as a man and they could see that he was subject to the same physical and emotional needs as themselves. It must have been difficult, if not impossible, for them to understand fully that Jesus was Lord of all and Son of God, until after the resurrection. Before that glorious revelation, when he was captured and crucified, their doubts must have come to the surface. Could this man really be as special as they had thought? Had they been deluding themselves? Indeed, had Jesus been deluding himself? By contrast, their delight and certainty after the resurrection and the absolute conviction that Jesus was Lord completely turned their lives up side down.

In some respects our own experience is like the experience of those first disciples. We know that Jesus was human. We can read about his words and actions in the Bible. We can have doubts about the miraculous elements in the gospel story. But then, like the disciples, we can become convinced that Jesus is our Lord and our lives can be completely changed. He is the Lord who understands us because he lived and died just as we do. He is the Lord who has power over all things, but yet empowers us to be free beings to do what we choose. He is the Lord who can speak to us in all sorts of ways if only we have the wit to listen to his voice. He is the Lord who is not only our divine creator, but is also our companion and our friend. He is the Lord who comes to us when we are lonely or hurt or lost. Yet, though he invites us to walk with him, he does not force us to do so. His love is all embracing, but at the same time full of concern that we should grow to our full stature emotionally and spiritually. To do this we need to be able to make our own decisions, though we can pray for guidance and advice. If you happen to have a boss at work who is at all like that, then you are very fortunate. Good parents and good teachers have some of these qualities, which are God given.

Questions for Discussion

○ *What was the importance of the Transfiguration?*
○ *Is the title "Lord" still appropriate today as a way of describing God or Jesus?*
○ *Why is the experience of Thomas the doubter so important to Christians?*

🐾 CHAPTER SEVEN 🐾

Conceived by the Holy Spirit

Human conception, as we all know, is the normal way of starting the process through which a baby is brought into the world. However, the Bible is unequivocal in saying that the male aspect of the conception of Jesus did not take place through Joseph or any other human being. For example, Matthew takes the trouble to find and quote a text from the prophet Isaiah to "prove" that the virgin birth was prophesied beforehand: *Look, the virgin shall conceive and bear a son, and they shall name him Emmanuel, which means 'God with us'* (Matthew 1:23 and see Isaiah 7:14). However, Matthew was using an ancient Greek translation of the Old Testament[12] which translates a Hebrew word meaning 'young woman' as *parthenos* (virgin). In other words, the original Isaiah text does not use the word for 'virgin'. When some people get to know this fact they immediately assume that the whole idea of the virgin birth must be untrue; but the truth of the story does not depend on this quotation from Isaiah. Matthew makes it quite clear that Joseph and Mary had not had a sexual relationship before she became pregnant and that Joseph was told by an angel what had really happened: . . . *an angel of the Lord appeared to him in*

---

[12] The Septuagint.

a dream and said, 'Joseph, son of David, do not be afraid to take Mary as your wife, for the child conceived in her is from the Holy Spirit [13] (Matthew 1:20).

Matthew is concerned about showing the fulfilment of Old Testament prophecy, which is why he uses the Isaiah quotation. He also emphasises that Joseph is of the house of David, which again is a fulfilment of Old Testament prophecy in that it was believed by the Jewish people that the Messiah would be a descendant of David. For example, the prophet Jeremiah writes: *The days are coming, says the Lord, when I will raise up for David a righteous Branch, and he shall reign as king . . . and this is the name by which he will be called 'The LORD is our righteousness'* (Jeremiah 23:5–6).

Luke also reports the miraculous conception of Jesus. Luke, in fact, uses the same word as Matthew (*parthenos*) to describe Mary's condition: *In the sixth month the angel Gabriel was sent by God to a town in Galilee called Nazareth, to a virgin engaged to a man whose name was Joseph, of the house of David. The virgin's name was Mary* (Luke 1:26–27). Like Matthew, Luke explains Mary's virginity very clearly. When Gabriel announces the conception of *the Son of the Most High* within Mary, her response is: *How can this be since I am a virgin?* [14] (Luke 1:34). According to Luke, a physician who must presumably have spoken to Mary, the angel then says: *The Holy Spirit will come upon you, and the power of the Most High will overshadow you; therefore the child to be born will be holy; he will be called the Son of God* (Luke 1:35).

The whole point of the virginal conception of Mary is that it is a sign from God to authenticate a special event, the

---

[13] The nature of the Holy Spirit is discussed in CHAPTER EIGHTEEN.

[14] The Greek here translates literally as, . . . *since I do not know a man.*

birth of God's Son as a human being, an event normally referred to as the Incarnation. According to the Bible God had given signs to people in past times. For example, when the prophet Isaiah announced beforehand to King Ahaz, through the Immanuel prophecy quoted above, that the Queen would have a baby, the prophet claimed his annunciation was a sign from God: *Therefore the Lord himself will give you a sign. Look, the young woman is with child and shall bear a son, and shall name him Immanuel* (Isaiah 7:14). The baby that was born became a famous and faithful king called Hezekiah. But was Isaiah not then speaking of the birth of the future Messiah, Jesus Christ? In fact, every Hebrew king was a messiah (an anointed one) so in that sense the prophet spoke of a messiah. However, he may well have been speaking at two levels, firstly to his own situation in eighth-century Judah, but also, perhaps unwittingly, to future generations. This could mean that God's word about the Incarnation was spoken by Isaiah, even though the prophet was not aware of the depth of meaning in his words. Matthew, as any rate, seems to have come to that conclusion and uses the Isaiah quotation to make the point.

Some people wonder why Saint Paul does not mention the Virgin Birth and therefore on that account question the authenticity of the story; but Paul was writing letters, not an account of the life of Jesus. However, he does write in his greeting to the Romans: . . . *the gospel according to his Son, who was descended from David according to the flesh and was declared to be Son of God with power according to the spirit of holiness by resurrection from the dead, Jesus Christ our Lord* (Romans 1:3–4). It seems that Paul emphasised the resurrection as God's sign that Jesus was His Son, whereas Luke emphasised the Virgin birth. It is worth noting that Paul and Luke were most probably friends and companions on some of Paul's missionary journeys. No doubt Luke would have shared with Paul his knowledge of the special birth of Jesus. Paul's silence on the matter does not mean he was not aware of it.

One awkward question is how Jesus could be descended from David if Joseph (of the tribe of David, see Luke 2:4) was not his natural father. Well, of course, silence about Mary's ancestry does not mean that she was not also of the tribe of David. Indeed, Luke specifically writes: . . . *and the Lord God will give to him the throne of his ancestor David* (Luke 1:32). Another possible conclusion is that Jesus was Joseph's son in the legal sense and was presumably recorded as such in the census mentioned in Luke 2:1–4. It is, of course, significant that Bethlehem, where Jesus was born, was traditionally the city of David (Luke 2:4).

What was God's purpose in sending his Son (coming himself) to be born of a virgin? It is generally thought that this was to announce the divinity of Jesus, as opposed to the humanity shown in his birth. As far as we know, and to be strictly accurate, Jesus had a normal human birth and it was Mary's conception through the Holy Spirit which was miraculous. As well as giving a sign to Mary and the world, it may be that this was also a sign for Jesus himself. No doubt Mary and Joseph told Jesus in due course of the way he had come into the world. As he grew he must have become aware that he had a unique vocation, and knowing of the way he entered human life he must have found spiritual strength to fulfil that vocation during his ministry and to complete it by his painful self-sacrifice on the cross.

To have faith in Christ is to trust in a God who not only signed his presence with a miracle, but also became one with us as a human being. When we share our concerns with God we are aware that he knows all about the problems of living and dying because he has been through the process himself. This is rather like the leader who claims that he will never ask his team to do anything he wouldn't do himself. God has done it himself. He's been there and done that. Of course God has always been there in the sense that he regards every one as his child and has always shared our experiences. What he did in the Incarnation was to make that abundantly clear to us, as if to say, *I am your God and I love you so much that I sent my Son to be one with you and to lead the way to me and to heaven. It was anything but easy to show my love for you in this way. But now you know. That is how deeply I love you all.* This, then, is the sort of God who is with us every step of the way throughout our lives whether we are aware of it or not. Those who do have the special insight to know this about God are very fortunate.

Questions for Discussion

○ *Is belief in the virgin birth necessary to be fully a Christian?*
○ *Do angels really exist?*
○ *Are all the miracles described in the Gospels true?*

CHAPTER EIGHT

Born of the Virgin Mary

As already pointed out, the birth of Jesus would have seemed normal to any observer, even though Mary was a virgin at the time of conception. So why did God choose a young and inexperienced girl to be Christ's mother? She way well have been very ordinary in her outward appearance, but her partially formed character must have been appropriate for the vocation she was presented with. The infallible judgement of God certainly decided that this was so. It is fascinating to think, from our present perspective, that the genes of Mary and her ancestors were repeated in the body of Christ. Despite the miracle of the conception Jesus was fully human: his bodily needs, his emotions, his capacity to reason, his curiosity, and so on, must have been similar to ours. In short, while his divinity was signed by the Holy Spirit, his humanity was signed by Mary.

It is surely important for us to know what we can about the Virgin Mary. What sort of person was the woman who brought God's Son to birth? While there is some information about her in other sources, the most appropriate place for us to learn what we can about her is in the Bible. From Luke's Gospel we may deduce that she was obedient to her call from God, transmitted to her through the angel Gabriel. After the Annunciation she said with great humility: *Here am I, the servant of the Lord; let it be with me according to your word* (Luke 1:37). Similarly, in Mary's Song (the Magnificat) her humility is described: . . . *for he (God) has looked with favour on the lowliness of his servant* (Luke 1:48).

It seems unlikely that Mary spoke the Magnificat to Elizabeth in its finished form. It is more probable that she expressed her feelings in simple words at the time and composed the song later.[15] Another possibility is that Luke wrote the song for her, basing it on her recollections. It is clear from the story of Mary's visit to her relation, Elizabeth, that both women were overjoyed at their respective pregnancies. It seems also that Elizabeth had a perception that Mary would be *the mother of my Lord* (Luke 1:43).

It is not surprising that the birth of Jesus and all the events associated with it should give Mary cause for serious thought (Luke 2:19). It is obvious that, despite her youth, she was having a deeply spiritual experience. Furthermore, she and Joseph were both keen to fulfil the law's requirements by having Jesus circumcised and by presenting him in the temple (Luke 2:21–36). It seems that Mary was a prayerful and conscientious Jewish girl. That she was a caring parent is confirmed by her concern when Jesus as a boy got lost while the family was on a pilgrimage to Jerusalem. She was also ready to rebuke the child because she was so worried (see Luke 2:41–51). Many parents today will recall similar experiences. Mary's normality is reassuring. It has to be remembered that the idealistic picture of Mary in the later history of the Church is based on deep reflection on her role in the Incarnation.

When Jesus began his ministry, his mother was aware of his miraculous powers, as illustrated in the story of the

---

[15] Unless she had written it before she went to see Elizabeth.

changing of water into wine at Cana: *When the wine gave out, the mother of Jesus said to him, 'They have no wine.' And Jesus said, 'Woman, what concern is that to you and to me? My hour has not yet come.' His mother said to the servants, 'Do whatever he tells you'* (John 2:3–5). The response of Jesus is puzzling, but Mary understands that he is willing to do something about the wine. From this it may be judged that the bond between mother and son was very strong. By contrast, there is another occasion when Jesus seems to distance himself from Mary and the family: *Then his mother and his brothers came and standing outside, they sent to him and called him. A crowd was sitting around him; and they said to him, 'Your mother and your brothers and sisters are outside, asking for you.' And he replied, 'Who are my mother and my brothers?' And looking at those who sat around him, he said, 'Here are my mother and my brothers. Whoever does the will of God is my brother and sister and mother'* (Mark 3:31–35). This suggests that Jesus is referring to a universal family of believers. Earlier in the same chapter we read that his family tried to restrain him because people were saying he was out of his mind (Mark 3:21) Luke tones down this same story, implying that Jesus could simply be saying that his mother and his family were models of faith (Luke 8:19–21). This is significant when we remember that Luke probably spoke at length with Mary when he learned about the background to the birth of Jesus.

Mary had been warned by the prophecy of Simeon of trouble to come. He said: . . . *a sword will pierce your own soul also* (Luke 2:35). When it came to watching her son die upon the cross, Simeon's prophecy must have hit her with its full meaning. Mary is not recorded in the gospels as having said anything at the cross, but Jesus showed his concern and love for her by binding Mary and John together in a new mother/son relationship: . . . *he said to his mother, 'Woman, here is your son.' Then he said to the disciple, 'Here is your mother.' From that hour the disciple took her into his own home* (John 19:26–27).

Mary's mourning was turned to joy, of course, when her son rose from the dead. While the gospels do not say so, we may imagine that Mary would be the first to see the risen Christ. Nothing further is said of Mary until Luke mentions her in his Acts of the Apostles. After the ascension of Jesus, she is described as being with the apostles leading a life of prayer: *All these were constantly devoting themselves to prayer, together with certain women, including Mary the mother of Jesus, as well as his brothers* (Acts 1:14). No doubt at this time Mary would ponder on her past life and perceive the deep implications of her vocation as the mother of God's Son.

There is a vast amount of literature about the Blessed Virgin Mary. There is also a range of views about her place in the Christian faith. These vary from a simple belief in what is told about her in the Bible, to veneration of Our Lady under many names. The creed, of course, speaks of the Communion of Saints, and whatever view is taken of Mary, it must surely be the case that she lives her life among the saints in fellowship with God's Son, her son. At the very least, her example of obedience to God's will and her humility provide an example to all Christians. Beyond the biblical view, some people believe that Mary is the Queen of Heaven and that she can intercede for people who ask for her help. Different Christian denominations express differing views on the subject. The Protestant view by and large holds that the Bible must be the guide about what we should believe about Mary. By contrast the Catholic Church has constructed several dogmas about the Virgin, the principal ones being the Immaculate Conception and the Assumption.[16]

Questions for Discussion

○ *Could Mary have refused her vocation to be the mother of Jesus?*

○ *How important is Mary in the story of the Incarnation?*

○ *What did Jesus mean when he said to his mother,* My hour has not yet come *(John 2:4)?*

---

[16] The Immaculate Conception expresses the view that Mary was free from all stain of original sin from the moment of her conception. The Assumption expresses the belief that Mary was assumed body and soul into heaven at the end of her earthly life. The Eastern Church celebrates a feast called the Dormition of the Virgin (i.e. the Falling Asleep).

CHAPTER NINE

*S*uffered under Pontius Pilate

Pontius Pilate was the governor or prefect of the Roman province of Judaea with his headquarters in Caesarea, not Jerusalem as many suppose. He is mentioned outside the Bible by at least two contemporary historians. He had a difficult job relating to the Jewish people and sometimes had to quell rebellions or pacify hostile Jewish leaders. This probably explains why he allowed Jesus to die, even though he knew him to be innocent. It was a political act.

The trial of Jesus was probably a routine matter for Pilate, who sat in judgement while the Jewish prosecutors presented their case, the high priest being their leader. Jesus had already been condemned by the Jewish Council (Sanhedrin) for admitting he was the Messiah (Matthew 26:63–66). One of the charges against Jesus, when he was dragged before the governor, was that he was forbidding people to pay taxes to the emperor (Luke 23:2). Jesus was questioned by Pilate, who asked him: *Are you the King of the Jews?* and Jesus replied: *You say so* (Matthew 27:11). To the governor's amazement, Jesus gave no further response to any of the accusations (Matthew 27:14). Pilate realised that Jesus was the victim of jealous and unfounded accusations. He decided that he would give the crowd the opportunity to release Jesus by following the custom at festival time of freeing a prisoner. He asked the crowd whether they wished to have Barabbas released, or *Jesus who is called the Messiah* (Matthew 27:17). The people called not only for the release of Barabbas, but shouted for the crucifixion of Jesus (Matthew 27:21–23).

John's Gospel gives more detail than the synoptic gospels[17] about the trial. According to John, when Jesus was asked if he was King of the Jews, he replied, *Do you ask this on your own, or did others tell you about me?* (John 18:34). Pilate replied that he was not a Jew, and that it was the Jewish leaders who had made the complaint. Then Pilate said, *What have you done?* The crux of Jesus' reply was, *My kingdom is not from this world.* At that Pilate asked him again, *So you are a king?* Jesus replied, *You say that I am a king. For this I was born, and for this I came into the world, to testify to the truth. Everyone who belongs to the truth listens to my voice.* Pilate then made his famous comment, *What is truth?* (see John 18:33–38) not realising that God's truth about life was being enacted before him

Although Pilate caved in to the demands of the Jewish leaders, he nevertheless recorded his belief in the innocence of Jesus by washing his hands publicly (Matthew 27:24). Jesus was then flogged and handed over to the soldiers who tortured him mercilessly before taking him to Golgotha: *They stripped him and put a scarlet robe on him, and after twisting some thorns into a crown, they put it on his head. They put a reed in his right hand and knelt before him, saying 'Hail, King of the Jews!' They spat on him and took the reed and struck him on the head* (Matthew 27:28–30).

The New Testament writers do not condemn Pilate

---

[17] Matthew, Mark and Luke, who all contain substantial material in common.

outright for his actions, but show that the blame for the death of Jesus was the responsibility of the Jewish leaders. Ironically, however, Pilate himself was later tried on serious charges and committed suicide.[18]

Pilate, of course, represented the supreme earthly authority in Judaea which was then part of the Roman Empire. He was supposed to promote justice, but like all politicians he was bound to take into account the political problems of the day. It seems that in the case of Jesus, Pilate's was a political decision. This means, however, that justice was not done and Pilate was fully aware that this was the case. How could he live with such a decision on his conscience? To be sure he did not realise that he was truly condemning the Son of God to a painful death, but to him it would be only one of many such judgements. Presumably he managed to live with his decisions by putting them at the back of his mind. Anyone who makes life or death decisions today must surely do the same, as if their lives can be divided into separate compartments. The alternative is to resign on the grounds of conscience. It can hardly be imagined that Pilate would have done that.

It is important to remember that Jesus, who was and is, at one with the Godhead, is therefore the supreme Judge of all human actions. Yet, in one particular place at one particular time in human history, he accepted the unjust judgement of a human court which condemned him to death. This shows that God not only came to earth as a human being, but that he came as a persecuted human being, which demonstrates the divine empathy with the

[18] According to a 3rd/4th century historian called Eusebius; see his "Ecclesiastical History", Book 2, Chapter 7, translated in *The Nicene and Post-Nicene Fathers*, Second Series, Vol. 1, ed. P. Schaff and H. Wace, T&T Clark, 1991 reprint.

millions of people who suffer unjust imprisonment, torture and painful death. Jesus became one of us, but not as a powerful politician or king. He came as a suffering human being, at one with the dregs of society. His suffering was real and extremely humiliating.

Of course, we may then ask why God chose to suffer in this way and why he allows so much suffering in the world. No one has been able to find a completely satisfactory answer to this question. However, it may be that the possibility of suffering is built into the lives of all of us for a good reason. If life was a bed of roses with no thorns, then would our essential characters and our spirits be able to develop and mature, ready for the next stage of life? It has to be admitted that this is one of life's great mysteries.

What is clear, is that anyone who is suffering pain or distress can turn to a God who has already been there himself. If our discomforts are minor ones, then we can accept that the suffering of Jesus was much greater than ours. On the other hand, if someone is suffering greatly, perhaps as a political prisoner, then he knows that Christ is with him every step of the way. This is God's supreme wisdom.

Questions for Discussion

○ *Why did God choose the particular time and place described in the Bible for the Incarnation?*

○ *Does human suffering have a meaning or a purpose?*

○ *How would you answer Pontius Pilate's question?* (What is truth?)

⤝ CHAPTER TEN ⤞

Crucified

Crucifixion was a common punishment in Greek and Roman times, initially reserved for disobedient slaves, and later for thieves and rebels. Sometimes hundreds of crucifixions took place simultaneously in order to deal with rebellions. There were different kinds of cross, but in all probability Jesus' cross would have had a strong vertical plank, already planted in the ground, and a cross bar which the victim was supposed to carry. On the other hand, it is possible that Jesus was made to carry the full cross. The fact that Jesus fell over when carrying his cross or bar may have been due to weakness caused by loss of blood during his torture. It was considered a great disgrace for anyone to undergo this sort of punishment. Death was slow and horrendous.[19]

Mark's Gospel records that a man called Simon of Cyrene was compelled to carry Jesus' cross (Mark 15:21). At Golgotha Jesus refused the offer of a drug, that is, wine mixed with myrrh, to ease his pain. At nine in the morning the crucifixion began. On the cross was posted the charge

[19] Those who wish to know more detail about the crucifixion should consult any good biblical encyclopedia, for example, *The International Standard Bible Encyclopedia*, Vol. One, ed. G. W. Bromiley et al., Eerdmans, 1980.

against Jesus in the words: *The King of the Jews.* Two robbers were crucified at the same time as Jesus. Passers-by made mocking remarks about his inability to save himself from the cross (see Mark 15:25–32). The whole country went dark around noon until three o'clock. Jesus then died with a loud cry. It was also reported that the curtain in the temple was torn into two pieces. A centurion who was watching came to the conclusion that Jesus was God's Son, possibly because of the things Jesus said (see below). Also watching from a distance were Mary Magdalene, Mary the mother of James, and Salome (see Mark 15:33–40).

Matthew adds some details to Mark's account. For example, he reports that some soldiers cast lots for Jesus' clothes and that there was an earthquake. He also states that tombs were opened and departed saints appeared in the town after the resurrection (see Matthew 27:35–56). In addition, Luke writes that a number of women from Jerusalem were following Jesus to his crucifixion and that they were weeping and wailing (Luke 23:27).

John's account adds further details which are not in the synoptic gospels. For example, he records that the charge against Jesus was written in Hebrew, Latin and Greek and that the chief priests asked Pilate to alter the wording from *The King of the Jews* to *This man said 'I am the King of the Jews'*, but Pilate refused. John also records that Jesus' mother and John the Apostle were at the foot of the cross. John the Evangelist (the same man?) reports that Jesus took some wine when he was thirsty, and that his side was pierced with a spear (see John 19:16–37).

When all the gospel accounts are put together, it is recorded that Jesus spoke seven times from the cross. These sayings are as follows:

My God, my God, why have you forsaken me?
                    (Matthew 27:46; Mark 15:34)
*Father, forgive them; for they do not know what they
    are doing*

                                        (Luke 23:34)
Truly I tell you, today you will be with me in Paradise
                                        (Luke 23:43)
Father, into your hands I commend my spirit
                                        (Luke 23:46)
Woman, here is your son. Here is your mother
                                        (John 19:26–27)

I am thirsty

                                        (John 19:28)

It is finished

                                        (John 19:30)

It seems that Luke and John had access to special
sources because they record sayings not mentioned by
Matthew and Mark. Luke may well have received some
information from the mother of Jesus; and if the author of
John's Gospel was the apostle John then, of course, he was
there at the foot of the cross with the Virgin Mary.

The sayings reveal a number of things. It is shown that
even in the extreme suffering of a painful death, Jesus
expressed concern and forgiveness for people, especially for
his mother. Jesus also deliberately showed the fulfilment of
an Old Testament prophecy in his quotation from Psalm 22
(*My God, my God . . .*). This is not to deny that Jesus felt
genuinely forsaken at the human level. The psalm, inci-
dentally, ends on a triumphal note. Jesus also showed his
complete humanity in his thirst, almost at the point of death.
One of the main points of the sacrifice of our Lord is shown
in his forgiveness of his enemies, for after all, it is through

the cross that all of us are forgiven. Despite his knowledge that he was God's Son, Jesus showed us how to pray at a time of need, by commending his spirit to God's care. He also showed the certainty of his faith in the promise to the thieves that they would join him in Paradise. Furthermore, he showed by the words, *It is finished*, not only that his life was ended, but also that his vocation as the Suffering Servant was fulfilled.

The symbol of the cross is very personal to all Christians. There is, first of all, the idea that we should take up the cross and follow Christ (see Matthew 10:38). This implies that we ought to accept our share of suffering without constant complaint and that we should be ever willing to suffer on behalf of others, in the name of Christ's love. Then there is the belief that the cross of Christ can transform us inwardly. Saint Paul saw his inner life as being transformed from the old self to the new self, through the cross and the resurrection (see Romans 6:1–4 and Galatians 5:22–25).

The reality of the cross, of course, is that Christ died so that we might literally live, that is, in a life beyond this one. As Saint Paul put it: *We know that Christ being raised from the dead, will never die again; death no longer has dominion over him* (Romans 6:9). And also: *For this perishable body must put on imperishability, and this mortal body must put on immortality* (1 Cor. 15:53). However, the symbolism of the cross in daily life is also important. For example, many people find it helpful to wear the symbol of the cross and this in itself is a kind of prayer, a commitment of themselves to the Lord's ultimate protection, whatever may happen to them. Furthermore, there is a sense in which every Christian must stand at the foot of Christ's cross in order to realise the full implications of what he did for each one of us.

Questions for Discussion

○ *Why crucifixion? Why didn't Jesus simply take over the world?*

○ *What is the value of the symbolism of the cross?*

○ *Did Jesus have a reason for quoting the first line of Psalm 22 while on the cross?*

Dead and Buried

The details of the burial of Jesus are intended to show that he was truly dead. Mark reports that the death was checked by a centurion, when Pilate asked for confirmation. It was the request of Joseph of Arimathea for the body of Jesus that motivated Pilate to confirm that death had actually taken place. Joseph was allowed to take the body and, after wrapping it in a linen cloth, he laid it in the tomb. A further important detail in Mark's account is that a stone was rolled across to block the door of the tomb. Two women, Mary Magdalene and Mary the mother of Joses observed the burial (see Mark 15:42–47).

Matthew adds to Mark's account an interesting detail about the tomb being especially sealed and guarded by soldiers at the request of the chief priests and Pharisees (Matthew 27:62–66). Luke mentions the fact that the tomb was hewn out of rock and that it had never been used previously for a burial (see Luke 23:50–55). John records that Nicodemus, a Pharisee who had visited Jesus secretly (John 3:1–10), brought a great weight of myrrh and aloes to be wrapped in layers of cloth around the body of Jesus. John also mentions that the new tomb was in a garden (see John 19:38–42).

There is, of course, an interesting prophetic parallel to

the death and burial of Jesus in the death and burial of Lazarus. Jesus delayed answering the call to come to his sick friend Lazarus and when he did arrive there was no doubt that Lazarus was dead. He had been in the tomb for four days, but yet Jesus called him back to life (see John 11:1–44). However, Lazarus was restored to normal human life, whereas the resurrection of Jesus restored him to his life beyond this world.

We all know that death will come to each one of us some day, and that our human remains will need to be disposed of. The historical reality of Jesus' death not only emphasises his humanity, but also shows that his remains were in some mysterious way reconstructed and joined to his spiritual body. Now it seems impossible that our remains may in some way come to life again, but that is the promise of the resurrection, which is discussed in CHAPTER TWENTY-ONE.

One of the puzzles of this life is why God created beings like ourselves who would age and die. Why couldn't he make us eternal to start with, instead of allowing us to go through the process of death before gifting us with eternal life? God surely emphasised the importance, in his view, of the mysterious value of death by going through the process himself. One reason may be, from our perspective, that we have the advantage of a completely new start in the next world, leaving behind all our failures and disappointments. Another reason which is sometimes suggested, may lie in the value of preparation for heaven through the many tribulations and trials we encounter here. Death itself is often a great tribulation and a painful way to go through the door to new life but, of course, the death of Christ was more painful than the passing that the majority of people experience.

Death is also a tribulation for those who are left behind to continue their lives here. This, too, may be part of the learning process for our immortal souls, to lose some one we love. In another sense, death brings loss to everyone because whatever treasures we may have acquired in this life we have to leave them behind. All we can take with us is the sort of person we have essentially grown to be. This may mean further hard lessons for those who have been entirely self-centred (see later on *judgement*).

The Bible makes it clear that Christ's victory over death was a signpost for us. God may have gifted us with a short life ending in death, but he also revealed to us through Christ that death, though awesome and frightening, is only a doorway to life. It was necessary for Jesus to be convincingly dead and securely buried for this message to have its full impact upon us.

Questions for Discussion

○ *What happened to the body of Jesus?*
○ *Do the contradictions in the Gospel stories about the resurrection matter?*
○ *Ought we to fear death?*

CHAPTER TWELVE

He Descended into Hell

Very few Christian doctrines are more controversial than the idea of hell. There are several biblical words which are associated with hell, or the place of the dead. The supposed location of hell is below the earth, but this is related to the three-level universe which people of ancient times accepted as the structure created by God. Heaven was envisaged as being "up there"; the earth was the level on which people lived; and hell or Hades was the lowest of the three levels (see Philippians 2:10 and Revelation 5:13). This view of the world is now seen as symbolic.

In the Old Testament Sheol was the name given to the underworld. This was the place of the dead over which God had sovereignty (see Psalm 139:8). It was sometimes seen as a place of punishment for the dead (Psalm 55:15). Later in this same psalm the writer describes God as consigning the wicked to the lowest pit (verse 23). In later Judaism, around the time of Jesus, it was envisaged that Sheol was divided into an abode for the wicked and another for the righteous (Enoch 22:1–14).

The New Testament describes an Abyss or bottomless pit where demons or people opposed to God live (see Luke 8:31). Saint Paul mentions the Abyss as the place of the dead (Romans 10:7). In the book of Revelation there is a picture of an abyss out of which the Beast or Anti-Christ (i.e. the devil) emerges to make war on the righteous (Revelation 11:7). However, the Beast and a false prophet are defeated and thrown into a lake of fire and sulphur (Revelation 19:11–21).

Another word used for hell in the New Testament is Hades. Hades, of course, was a pagan god who was lord of the underworld. The name came to be used universally for the place of the dead. According to the Bible, Christ has the keys to Hades (Revelation 1:18). Furthermore, Christ told Peter (who was given the keys of heaven) and the other disciples that the gates of Hades would not prevail against the Church (Matthew 16:18). Among other things this may mean that Christ had conquered death and so the Church would safeguard its people from death. Some texts imply that with Christ's victory over Hades, the stay of people there would be temporary (see Acts 2:27, 31). However the parable of Jesus about Dives and Lazarus may imply that consignment to Hades is eternal (Luke 16:19–31).

Another word used in connection with the idea of hell is Gehenna. This is interpreted as a place of eternal, fiery punishment. For example, in his Sermon on the Mount, Jesus says that those deserving judgement will be *liable to the hell of* fire (Matthew 5:22 and see Mark 9:43). According to Matthew, Jesus also states that both body and soul can be destroyed in hell (Matthew 10:28).

Some of the problems about the idea of hell include the following:

Is it a place or a state of being?
Are people really there for eternity?
How does hell square with God's love?
Is there a halfway house before judgement?

Do non-Christians go to hell regardless?

What is the purpose of hell?

Is the punishment by fire literal or symbolic language?

Is hell simply separation from God?

Can people in hell repent?

Do people go to hell (or heaven) when they die or after Judgement Day?

Is the pain of hell spiritual or sensory?

Is there a purgatory (remedial and temporary)?

What happens to unbaptised infants? Is there a limbo for them?

It would take a full book to attempt to answer these questions, which are listed here mainly to emphasise the problems associated with Christ's descent to hell. The idea of such a descent is based on certain biblical texts. For example, according to Matthew, at the time of the death of Jesus, the tombs were opened and bodies of the saints *who had fallen asleep* were raised and appeared to numerous people (Matthew 27:52f.). Did Christ, then, visit the place of the dead where saints and sinners were all waiting? Luke records some words of Jesus to the penitent thief while the crucifixion took place: *Truly I tell you, today you will be with me in paradise* (Luke 23:43). Yet again it seems to be clear that Jesus believed he was going to the place of the dead. The thief, however, who might have been expected to go to hell, was promised a place in paradise. More specifically, Peter reports in his first letter: *He (Jesus) was put to death in the flesh, but made alive in the spirit, in which also he went and made a proclamation to the spirits in prison, who in former times did not obey . . .* (1 Peter 3:18–20). Peter seems to have believed that Jesus went to the place of the punishment of the dead, the prison beyond the grave. This is a recognisable description of what we generally mean by hell.

In medieval times the notion of the "harrowing of hell" came to prominence. This process is usually taken to refer to the conquest of devilish and evil powers when Christ descended into hell. One of the meanings of the word "harrow" is "to torment someone" while another meaning is "to plunder". Thus, it is implied that the evil powers of hell were inflicted on evil beings who underwent great suffering.

But what, in plain English, does Christ's descent into hell mean? First of all it means that he was really dead. Secondly, it means that before the resurrection he actually visited the place of the dead. Thirdly, it shows that Christ is all powerful, even in hell in the company of evil beings. This means that evil and death were defeated by suffering love.

Questions for Discussion

○ *Choose three questions from the list given above.*

CHAPTER THIRTEEN

The Third Day He Rose Again From the Dead

The evidence for the resurrection is to be found in the Bible and in the continuing tradition of the Church. Possibly the earliest mention of the resurrection in the New Testament is in Paul's first letter to Corinth. He writes: *For I handed on to you as of first importance what I in turn had received: that Christ died for our sins in accordance with the scriptures, and that he was buried, and that he was raised on the third day according to the scriptures, and that he appeared to Cephas (Peter), then to the twelve. Then he appeared to more than five hundred brothers and sisters at one time, most of whom are still alive . . .* (1 Corinthians 15:3–6). This is strong testimony from a man who persecuted the Church before his conversion. Most scholars date this letter to around the mid-fifties AD. The Gospels, in which most of the detailed evidence is set out, were probably written between AD 65–100, though opinion on the dating is constantly shifting. At any rate, the evangelists were writing of events that happened thirty or more years previously; but are their recollections accurate? It is a fact that many people today can remember clearly events which happened, say, fifty years ago. In the same way, especially for something as vivid as the resurrection, there must have been many people, as Paul claims, who could remember what happened decades later.

Of course it is obvious from a careful comparison that the four Gospels differ in the details. However, on the main message they all agree. The tomb was empty and the risen Jesus appeared to a number of people, some of them named. Matthew reports that Mary Magdalene and the other Mary saw the empty tomb (Matthew 28:1). Mark mentions Salome as one of the women (Mark 16:1), while Luke mentions Joanna and other women (Luke 24:10). John, on the other hand, places the emphasis on Mary Magdalene followed by a visit to the tomb by Peter and John (John 20:1–4). These accounts do not necessarily contradict each other because, if there were other women as well as those named, as Luke suggests, then the evangelists have probably emphasised different details of the same event.

There are also differences in the report of an angel or angels at the tomb. Matthew describes an angel with an appearance like lightning (Matthew 28:2–3). Mark describes a young man in white (Mark 16:5). Luke mentions two men in dazzling clothes (Luke 24:4). John mentions two angels in white (John 20:12). Two of the evangelists, then, record that there was one angelic being (divine messenger) at the tomb, while the other two evangelists record that there were two such angelic beings. One possible explanation for this difference in the accounts could be that the witnesses were scared out of their wits, and some believed they had seen one angel whereas in fact there may have been two, or vice versa. Another possible explanation could be that one angel appeared first and that another appeared later. A further explanation could be that the women were each having a vision and that their perceptions were different. What all the evangelists agree upon was that there was at least one special appearance by a divine messenger.

Matthew and Luke seem to share material from Mark, whereas John contains a lot of resurrection stories not in the other Gospels. For example, John provides us with these stories: Mary Magdalene in the garden (cf. Mark 16:9–11); Doubting Thomas, Jesus meeting the disciples by the lake; the charge to Peter and mention of the beloved disciple (see John 20–21). If the author of John's Gospel was the apostle John, the beloved disciple, this would explain why he knew what happened in such vivid detail. Alternatively, if John was not the author, he could have told these stories to the author. Luke's unique contribution is the story of the two disciples on the road to Emmaus, though this seems to be mentioned briefly in Mark (see Luke 24:13–35 and Mark 16:12–13). Again, these difference are a question of emphasis rather than contradiction.

What is odd about the appearances of the risen Jesus is that some seem "ghostly" while others seem very physical. An apparent example of the first type is recorded by John when he reports that Jesus suddenly appeared to the disciples in a house where the doors were locked (John 20:19–23). Jesus, however, according to Luke, emphasises that he is not a ghost and that the disciples should touch him. Then Jesus is reported as eating a piece of fish (Luke 24:39–43). Moreover, John also records that Thomas actually touched the body of Jesus (John 20:27). To complicate things further, Jesus asked Mary Magdalene, who had not at first recognised him, not to touch him or hold on to him because he had not yet ascended to the Father (John 20:17). This may mean, however, that Jesus was saying that his earthly connections would have to be broken, not that Mary was not to touch him physically. It is also strange that the two disciples on the road to Emmaus did not recognise Jesus until he broke bread at the table, blessed and broke it, and gave it to them (Luke 24:30–31). Of course, if you believe a person is dead, then you do not expect to meet him while you are out walking, so that could be sufficient explanation of what happened. The breaking of bread is a reference surely to communion, and this may have been a point when Jesus wished to show, through a further revelation, that he would be with the disciples when they broke the bread which would become his body.

The nature of Christ's risen body as he appeared to the witnesses is mysterious. Also, what happened to the body in the tomb? It can only be surmised that somehow, by God's almighty power, the earthly body of Jesus was transmuted into his heavenly body. Certainly, the body of the risen Jesus which people saw, bore the wounds of his crucifixion (John 20:27). However, as already noted, the risen Jesus could appear how and where he willed, even revealing himself in a locked house (John 20:19). Did the disciples have some kind of vision or was the risen Jesus objective, in the sense that anyone present could have seen him or touched him? In the end we have to rely upon the testimony of the witnesses, as transmitted through the evangelists. If the resurrection did not truly take place, it is difficult to see how the Church could have been founded. After all, the disciples must have been at rock bottom after the death of their Lord. Yet, within weeks, if not days, their spirits were lifted and they began to break bread together in the belief that Christ was present with them.

One interesting fact about the resurrection appearances of Jesus is that he gave his disciples instructions to follow. Mark reports Jesus as saying: *Go into all the world and proclaim the good news to all creation* (Mark 16:15). Matthew's version of this instruction is somewhat different: *Go therefore and make disciples of all nations, baptising them in the name of the Father and of the Son and of the Holy Spirit* (Matthew 28:19). Luke writes: . . . *repentance and forgiveness of sins is to be proclaimed in his name to all nations, beginning from Jerusalem* (Luke 24:47). John, in a similar vein, writes: *Peace be with you. As the Father has sent me, so I send you* (John 20:21). The risen Jesus said much more than that, but the examples quoted show a measure of agreement, even though the wording is different.

One of the problems in trying to come to some assessment of the accuracy of what the evangelists write, not only about the resurrection, but in general, is that the accounts have probably gone through a process of oral tradition, some sharing of sources, some editing possibly at a later time. One interesting aspect of this problem is that Mark and John seem to have alternative endings to their gospels. For example, Mark has a short ending or a longer ending, and many scholars believe that Mark 16:9–20 are a later addition. Similarly, in John's Gospel, Chapter 20:30–31 seem to conclude the Gospel and therefore many conclude that Chapter 21 has been added later, either by the author himself or by another hand. Despite all these difficulties, it is apparent to many theologians that the Holy Spirit has guided the writers and editors of the New Testament so that they have produced a set of documents which outline the truth about God's revelation. Jesus Christ was God incarnate and he rose from the dead before many witnesses. That is the Christian proclamation.

Questions for Discussion

○ *Do the contradictions in the resurrection stories matter?*
○ *What will the resurrection life be like?*
○ *How reliable is the testimony of the first witnesses?*

⤛ CHAPTER FOURTEEN ⤜

He Ascended Into Heaven

Matthew's Gospel and John's Gospel do not mention the ascension of Jesus into heaven. Mark's Gospel reports briefly: *So then the Lord Jesus, after he had spoken to them, was taken up into heaven and sat down at the right hand of God* (Mark 16:19). Luke's Gospel is equally brief: *While he was blessing them, he withdrew from them and was carried up into heaven* (Luke 24:51). However, some ancient manuscripts of Luke omit the words *and was carried up into heaven*. It is possible, then, that an editor or scribe added these words to harmonise Luke's Gospel with Luke's history, that is, Acts of the Apostles.[20] Indeed, it is in the book of Acts that we read of the Ascension in some detail (see Acts 1:6–11).

The main points in Luke's description in Acts are as follows: the last appearance of Jesus happens on the Mount of Olives (see v.12); the coming of the Holy Spirit is promised; the disciples are promised that through the power of the Holy Spirit they will be Christ's witnesses across the earth; Christ is lifted up and is concealed by a cloud; two men dressed in white announce that Jesus will come again.

The similarities of the Ascension to the descriptions of

[20] Most authorities assume that Luke wrote both the Gospel and Acts.

the Transfiguration are noteworthy. Mark, for example, reports that two men appear with Jesus (Elijah and Moses) and that a cloud conceals them and Jesus. Then suddenly Jesus is seen alone (Mark 9:2–8). The Transfiguration also took place on a mountain (possibly Tabor or Hermon).

What both stories do quite plainly is describe a link between heaven and earth. The inhabitants of heaven (one aspect of the existence beyond this one) appear at critical times. This also happens at the empty tomb, as mentioned earlier in this book in connection with the resurrection (see Mark 16:5 for example). This link is only an up and down one in a symbolic sense, as in the story of Jacob's ladder (Genesis 28:12). The word Ascension is therefore symbolic of a move from earth into the spirit world from which Jesus "descended" to earth in the Incarnation.

The experiences of the witnesses who saw these visitors from beyond may have been visionary, though this does not make them any the less real. If some bystanders had been around when the Ascension took place, they could have been blind to what was happening. Of course, the Bible insists that the risen Jesus could be touched, so these other people, or angels, who appeared could possibly have had been apparent in a full physical sense. It seems much less likely that the stories of these appearances are merely imaginary symbols used by the evangelists to make their stories more meaningful.

The promise that Jesus would *come in the same way* as he had been seen going into heaven (Acts 1:11) indicates that the work of Christ was incomplete. The early disciples certainly expected Jesus to return. This is further testimony to the coming and going which God allows between heaven and earth. The Ascension, then, was an *au revoir*, not a final goodbye. The coming of the Holy Spirit at Pentecost, also promised at the Ascension, is another example of God revealing himself and allowing a special communication from heaven to strike selected witnesses in a spectacular way.

The Ascension account clearly brings to an end the appearances of the risen Jesus and an end to the Incarnation. One chapter of the divine revelation is shown to have ended, but further chapters are announced beforehand. The story is both an epilogue and a prologue. We are invited "to watch this space". That is an invitation which is always there. God is constantly revealing himself in all kinds of ways to all kinds of people.

We live in a world where there are pathways or ladders to heaven. This is true in the ultimate sense, in that each of us has to go through an Ascension or departure to the next life. It is also true in the immediate sense, in that messengers or angels are immersed in our daily lives and bring tidings or guidance from God. From our human perspective, our prayers and actions are messages which go the other way, from earth to heaven. It may be asked, of course, why such frequent and regular two-way spiritual activity is not apparent or convincing to everybody. Only God knows the answer to that question. However, if doubters attempt to link into the system they may well have a pleasant surprise.

Questions for Discussion

○ *Read Genesis 28:10–22. What is the meaning of Jacob's vision?*

○ *Read 2 Kings 2:1–12. Was the chariot of fire a piece of symbolism or did Elisha see a chariot?*

○ *Read Revelation 21:1–4. Will heaven on earth ever be possible?*

$\int itting$ at the Right Hand of God

At his trial before the high priest, Jesus is asked, *Are you the Messiah, the Son of the Blessed One? Jesus said, I am, and you will see the Son of Man seated at the right hand of the Power, and coming with the clouds of heaven* (Mark 14:61–62). It was this statement that brought about our Lord's condemnation to death. There are numerous other descriptions in the New Testament of Christ in glory at the Father's right hand. One of the most significant is described in the account of Stephen's death: *But filled with the Holy Spirit, he gazed into heaven and saw the glory of God and Jesus standing at the right hand of God* (Acts 7:55).

Peter, in his Pentecost sermon, testifies to his belief in Christ's glory and at the same time mentions Christ's relationship to the Father and the Holy Spirit: *Being therefore exalted at the right hand of God, and having received from the Father the promises of the Holy Spirit, he has poured out this that you both see and hear* (Acts 2:33).

From the texts quoted above together with a number of other texts, it is clear that the creed bases its statement that Christ is *sitting at the right hand of God* on biblical sources. However, this affirmation of Christ's glory ought not to be interpreted literally. The essential meaning of the phrase is that Christ has a specially relationship with God, and that he shares the glory of God. The importance of this idea for each one of us is that we too are drawn into God's glory by the humanity of Christ. It is true that in this life most of us catch only glimpses of the glory of the Trinity. However, John's Gospel is certain that in contemplating the Christ of the Incarnation, we are beholding the divine glory. In his prologue John writes: *And the Word became flesh and lived among us, and we have seen his glory, the glory as of a father's only son, full of grace and truth* (John 1:14). This is poetic language, but it demonstrates a great truth – God was in the human Christ, and Christ is in the glory of God. There is a sense in which the divine glory is in each of us now, a seed that will flower when we move to the next stage of existence.

This does not sound like a very practical idea, but it does impinge on our daily lives. Our future hopes and our dreams of heaven are what inspire us to live our lives close to God. Furthermore, the glory of God is like a beacon which leads us on to the gates of the heavenly Jerusalem. There Christ himself will meet us and he will clothe us in his glorious light. Yes, he is sitting at the right hand of God, and yes, he is expecting us.

Questions for Discussion

○ *Read Daniel 7:13–14. In what ways has this prophecy come true?*
○ *Why did God allow a faithful servant like Stephen to be martyred?*
○ *Is it possible to perceive some element of God's glory in the here and now? How?*

⊰ CHAPTER SIXTEEN ⊱

Judging the Living and the Dead

The idea of judgement before God is an uncomfortable one. Yet we have to face up to the idea that judgement is a common theme in the Bible. As is well known, the Old Testament prophets mention the idea of judgement frequently, especially against those who are guilty of cruelty or social injustice (see for example Isaiah 5; Jeremiah 9; Amos 5). Likewise, in the New Testament, judgement of bad behaviour is a central topic in the gospels, in the letters and in the Book of Revelation (see for example Mark 13; Romans 2; Revelation 16). Such biblical passages do not make easy reading.

Of the many parables Jesus told, several are about divine judgement. One of the best known of such stories is the parable of the sheep and the goats (Matthew 25:31–46). According to Matthew's account, the Son of man will come and sit upon his glorious throne. All peoples will gather before his throne and they will be separated into two groups, the sheep to his right hand and the goats to his left. The sheep are the ones who will inherit eternity because they have cared for those in dire need. The goats are the ones who will go into eternal punishment because they have not helped those in trouble or need. This is a clear prophecy by our Lord himself that he will return one day to judge the world. Other parables of judgement include: the dragnet (Matthew 13:47–50); the unforgiving servant (Matthew 18:23–35); the wicked tenants (Matthew 21:33–44); the weeds and the wheat (Matthew 13:24–30).

There is some ambiguity in the New Testament about whether it is the Father or the Son who judges the world. For example, in 1 Peter 1:17 we read: *If you invoke as Father the one who judges all people impartially according to their deeds, live in reverent fear during the time of your exile.* At the same time there are several statements that it is the Son who will judge the world. In Paul's second letter to Corinth 5:10 we read: *For all of us must appear before the judgement seat of Christ, so that each may receive recompense for what has been done in the body, whether good or evil.* Saint Paul also writes: *In the presence of God and of Christ Jesus, who is to judge the living and the dead . . .* (2 Timothy 4:1). In other places only the word God is used to identify the judge. Paul writes: *For we will all stand before the judgement seat of God* (Romans 14:10). Of course, if God is truly a Trinity there is no ultimate contradiction in these statements. Furthermore, the New Testament writers were groping to find the correct language to describe indescribable mysteries – just as we are today.

There is strong evidence that the first Christians expected Christ to come again during their lifetime. For example, Paul writes: *For this we declare to you by the word of the Lord, that we who are alive, who are left until the coming of the Lord, will by no means precede those who have died* (1 Thessalonians 4:15). Paul goes on to say that the faithful dead will rise and then the living will be taken up to heaven to be with Christ. James also writes: *Strengthen your hearts, for the coming of the Lord is near* (James 5:8). Of course, we now know that Christ did not appear again in the first century AD, but nevertheless his second coming is so strongly attested in the New Testament that it is a central tenet of Christian teaching.

In Paul's description of the Lord's Supper he writes, *For as often as you eat this bread and drink the cup, you proclaim the Lord's death until he comes* (1 Corinthians 11:26). This, of course, is what the Church is still doing in its regular celebration of communion. At the end of that first letter to Corinth Paul prays for the Lord's coming: *Our Lord, come! (Marana tha)* (1 Corinthians 16:22). This is a good prayer for all Christians and it can be used in the immediate sense of crying to God for help, or in the ultimate sense of hoping Christ will come again soon. This is similar to the statement in the book of Revelation: *I am coming soon; hold fast to what you have, so that no one may seize your crown* (Revelation 3:11).

Only a few of the many biblical statements about Christ's coming and the final judgement have been quoted above to show that what the creed says is soundly based in scripture. However, we are then faced with the problem of interpretation. What is involved in God's judgement? Are people sent to eternal damnation or to heavenly eternity, and is there a place between these two extremes? The parable of Jesus about the rich man and Lazarus indicates that we need to take the idea of judgement very seriously (see Luke 16:19–31). The rich man, who has led a selfish life, ends up in eternal torment; whereas the poor man, Lazarus, is carried away by angels to live with Abraham. There is no escape for the rich man and he cannot even warn his brothers about the punishment that is awaiting them.

It may be, of course, that the language used about heaven and hell is symbolic (see CHAPTER TWELVE).

However, what is clear is that each of us will have to give an account of our lives before God. In a sense, that happens already each day if we take our prayers seriously and ask for forgiveness of our wrongdoings. We can be very much aware of any hurt we may have caused other people, and the guilt can be quite painful. Such contemplation of our misdeeds may well be a taste of what hell is like. In other words, in relation to judgement, hell may be a state of mind, not a geographical location. Similarly, heaven may also be a state of mind or a state of being.

However, our experiences in this life may be a guide to what happens in the next life. Many people learn from their experiences and modify their behaviour because they do not wish to hurt people as they may have done in the past. Some people, on the other hand, do not seem to develop in the moral sense and live completely selfish lives. It is difficult for us to make such judgements, of course, because only God knows the whole picture. Nevertheless, there does appear to be a process of development and understanding in our relationships with people and with God. It is difficult to believe that this process is simply cut off when we transfer to the next life. Logic and common sense indicate that our learning experiences will continue and that where we have failed we may have to learn hard lessons, though always in the context of God's love. The judgement we have to face may then resemble a school report or a job evaluation. Where are you up to? and where do you go from here? may be relevant questions. In a sense also, the judgement must involve judgement of ourselves, though this must surely be in relation to the consistent moral standards revealed by God.

Those who believe in a God who has created a world with moral dimensions must surely take the idea of an ultimate judgement very seriously. Whether the judgement takes place immediately after passage into the next world or on a great Judgement Day for all, is an open question. God does not choose to allow us to penetrate too deeply into the mysteries of life after death.

Questions for Discussion

○ *Is hell eternal?*
○ *Are mercy and judgement contradictory?*
○ *Have we the right to forgive serious crimes like murder?*

⊰ CHAPTER SEVENTEEN ⊱

I Believe in the Holy Spirit

The Holy Spirit was involved in the two most important events in our universe (at least that we are aware of). These were God's creation and the Incarnation. The parts played by the Holy Spirit in these two events are discussed above in chapters THREE and SEVEN, respectively. Apart from these two acts of God, another main revelation concerning the Holy Spirit took place on the Day of Pentecost, when God introduced himself in this capacity in an amazing way to selected disciples of the departed Jesus (see Acts 2:1–4).

Our Lord himself was very conscious of the working of the Spirit during his Incarnation. For example, when he read the lesson in the synagogue in Nazareth, his home town, he chose to read a passage from Isaiah beginning with the words: *The Spirit of the Lord is upon me . . .* (Luke 4:18 and Isaiah 61:1). Jesus' comment on the reading was: *Today this scripture has been fulfilled in your hearing* (Luke 4:21). Also, describing the baptism of Jesus, Luke reports that *the Holy Spirit descended upon him in bodily form like a dove* (Luke 3:22).

Furthermore, Jesus promised that he would send the Advocate[21] (helper) or the Spirit of truth to his disciples

---

[21] Sometimes translated as "Paraclete" from the Greek *paraklētos*.

(John 16:5–15). Jesus said: *When the Spirit of truth comes, he will guide you into all truth, for he will not speak on his own, but will speak whatever he hears, and he will declare to you the things that are to come* (John 16:13). In the same vein, Luke reports that the risen Jesus said: *And see, I am sending upon you what my Father promised; so stay here in the city until you have been clothed with power from on high* (Luke 24:49). Jesus then foretold that God's Holy Spirit would both guide the disciples and give them power. Certainly, in the early Church, as described in Acts of the Apostles, the Holy Spirit clearly fulfils the promise of Jesus. For that reason the book of Acts is sometimes called the Gospel of the Holy Spirit.

As examples of the Holy Spirit's guidance, several stories may be mentioned. When Saul and Barnabas were at Antioch *the Holy Spirit said, "Set apart for me Barnabas and Saul for the work to which I have called them* (Acts 13:2). The Holy Spirit also sometimes spoke against certain actions. Paul and Silas for instance, were *forbidden by the Holy Spirit to speak in Asia* (Acts 16:6–7). Later in the book Paul says: . . . *the Holy Spirit testifies to me in every city that imprisonment and persecutions are waiting for me* (Acts 20:23).

The power of the Holy Spirit is illustrated in several parts of the book, in addition to what happened on the Day of Pentecost. For example, the members of the church prayed for help and the Holy Spirit responded: *When they had prayed, the place in which they were gathered together was shaken; and they were all filled with the Holy Spirit and spoke the word of God with boldness* (Acts 4:31). The Holy Spirit as Comforter is also attested: *Meanwhile the church throughout Judea, Galilee, and Samaria had peace and was built up. Living in the fear of the Lord and in the comfort of the Holy Spirit, it increased in numbers* (Acts 9:31). An example of the Holy Spirit in direct action through Paul is given in the story of the mission to Cyprus. Paul made an enemy of Bar-Jesus there, *but Saul, also known as Paul, filled with the Holy Spirit, looked intently at him and said, "You son of the devil . . . the hand of the Lord is against you and you will be blind for a while . . .* The man was immediately without sight (Acts 13:9–11).

Another interesting manifestation of the work of the Spirit involves people who felt themselves to be inspired by the Spirit. For example, the prophet Ezekiel, when he believed God was speaking through him, wrote: *Then the Spirit of the Lord fell on me . . .* (Ezekiel 11:5). In a similar way the author of the Book of Revelation felt inspired and wrote: *I was in the Spirit on the Lord's day . . .* (Revelation 1:10). It is important to remember that the Holy Spirit was at work up to and including the time of Christ as well as after the Day of Pentecost.

Saint Paul is very conscious in his letters of the importance of recognising both the fruits of the Spirit and the gifts of the Spirit. He lists the fruits of the Spirit as: *love, joy, peace, patience, kindness, generosity, faithfulness, gentleness and self control* (Galatians 5:22–23). In another letter he shows that there are varieties of gifts in the Spirit, and lists, for example, wisdom, knowledge faith, healing, miracle working, prophecy, discernment of spirits and interpretation of tongues (1 Corinthians 12:4–11).

Volumes could be written about what the Bible says concerning the Holy Spirit. However, only a brief summary is given here. Perhaps the final word should be granted to Paul, who yet again shows wonderful insight: *If we live by the Spirit, let us also be guided by the Spirit* (Galatians 5:25).

Of course, the question for us today is just how do we live by the Spirit? As Jesus himself said, *The wind (Spirit) blows where it chooses* (John 3:8). In other words, we cannot control the Spirit. However, we can pray for the help of God's Holy Spirit and we may receive the same sort of power and guidance as the people of the early Church. Certainly, many people today can testify to having had some experience of help from the Holy Spirit. The fruits of the Spirit as described by Saint Paul are unchanging values. If we are living by the Spirit then we ought to bear the fruits of the Spirit. No doubt also the gifts of the Spirit we may recognise today include those outlined by Paul, but in addition to those, there are numerous gifts which may be added to Paul's list. For example, people who can organise or plan events for their congregation are often inspired by the Spirit. People who clean the church or arrange the flowers often have a special gift for service. People who are involved in pastoral care are also using a gift from God, as are those who express their faith through the arts or literature. The same principle applies to our use in the service of Christ of any of the gifts or talents which God has given us.

The Holy Spirit, then, is God's way of acting in the world. God is not a distant, absentee figure. He is directly involved in our affairs and he calls us through the Spirit to serve him and to serve the community in which we live.

Questions for Discussion

○ *How does the Holy Spirit manifest himself today?*
○ *What are the gifts of the Spirit in today's Church?*
○ *How would you explain the idea of the Holy Spirit to non-believers?*

CHAPTER EIGHTEEN

The Holy Catholic Church

The creed expresses the thought that we believe in *the Church*. So what is the Church? It is not a collection of church buildings, but rather a collection of people. This may be illustrated by comparing a household with a house, the former referring to people and the latter to the building. Paul, in fact, in writing to Timothy, refers to *the household of God which is the church of the living God* (1 Timothy 3:15). In the New Testament, the usual Greek word translated as "church" is *ekklēsia*,[22] which literally means "called out" and the word was used in classical Greek to refer to gatherings of citizens. Of course, in the New Testament it refers to the gathering of God's people. This can be general, that is universal, or it can be particular, that is with reference to a local church. However, when it is used of a local church, the implication is that the congregation in that place are part of the great gathering of all God's people. An interesting use of the word is recorded in Paul's letter to Colossae. Paul writes of a woman called Nympha and *the church in her house* (Colossians 4:15). Yet again, in his letter to the Romans Paul writes: *All the churches of Christ greet you* (Romans 16:16). Moreover, according to Matthew, Jesus himself

---

[22] The word "ecclesiastical" is derived from this Greek word.

uses the word *ekklēsia* when he says to Peter: . . . *you are Peter, and on this rock I will build my church . . .* (Matthew 16:18). The apostles, of course, and other disciples, did just that. They gathered together people who had faith in Christ. The process continues, and the faithful down to this very day, constitute the Church.

The Church is also Catholic. The first Christian writer who is known to have used the word *katholikos* (catholic) of the Church is Saint Ignatius of Antioch (*c.* AD 35–107). He writes: . . . *wherever Jesus Christ is, there is the Catholic Church* (Epistle to Smyrna, Chapter eight).[23] The word "catholic" means "general" or "universal". Of course, the word is used in non-religious contexts with this meaning. For example, somebody might say, *I have catholic tastes in literature.* However, the word has come to have a range of meanings in the Church. For example, as well as referring to the Roman Church, it can be used of the universal Church as opposed to local congregations. It is also some-times used to describe those groups with orthodox beliefs, rather than heretical ones. Sometimes it is used to describe groups of Christians who have a continuous tradition from apostolic times.[24] However, the original meaning of the word "catholic" in the creed was probably "universal", referring to all gatherings of Christians.

The Church is also holy. The word "holy" of course, is used frequently in the Bible. In the Hebrew (OT) the word is thought to have a root meaning of "separateness", though there are other theories about the origin of the concept. The part of the Jerusalem temple separated as very special was

---

[23] See *The Ante-Nicene Fathers*, Vol. 1, ed. A. Roberts and J. Donaldson, T & T Clark, 1996 reprint.
[24] See *The Oxford Dictionary of the Christian Church*, ed. F. L. Cross and E. A. Livingstone, Oxford University Press, 1997.

called the Holy of Holies. In a similar way, in many churches, the sanctuary behind the altar rail is regarded as especially holy, that is separated for closeness to God. The main word for "holy" used in the New Testament (*'agios)* seems to have been used outside the Bible to mean "awe inspiring". This idea also implies the idea of separateness or otherness. The important point is that in the Bible and in the Church, people, things and places came to be regarded as holy because of their association with awe-inspiring experiences of the holiness of God.

So it is that the people of God are called to holiness. In fact, the New Testament borrows this idea from the Old Testament. In the Old Testament, for example, the Book of Leviticus reads: *For I am the Lord your God; sanctify your-selves therefore, and be holy, for I am holy* (Leviticus 11:44 and see v. 45). The first Letter of Peter quotes from the Book of Leviticus: . . . *for it is written, "You shall be holy, for I am holy"* (1 Peter 1:16). This means that the people of God, that is the Catholic Church, should accept the pursuit of holiness as part of the Christian vocation. Striving to be holy not only means living close to the holy God, it also has an ethical dimension. Righteousness and love are insepa-rable from holiness.

What then, in ordinary language, does the phrase *Holy Catholic Church* mean? The phrase could be rewritten as *all the followers of Christ trying to be like him.* In everyday terms this is not an easy vocation. However, that is what the Christian life is about. Inevitably we make mistakes, falling short of perfection, failing to be as holy as we are called to be. But in our membership of the Holy Catholic Church we also have access to God's love and forgiveness. There is a balance between striving for righteousness and holiness on the one hand, and reconciliation between ourselves and the holy God on the other hand. To the outsider this may sound like a boring and humourless sort of life, but the reality is exciting, challenging, and sometimes rather amusing. It is a wonderful experience to belong to the Holy Catholic Church.

Questions for Discussion

○ *In view of differences in practice and in some aspects of doctrine can the Church ever be truly catholic?*
○ *Which is the most holy Christian place? Why?*
○ *How would you explain what the Church is to an alien from another galaxy?*

CHAPTER NINETEEN

The Communion of Saints

Saints (the holy ones) are mentioned in both Old and New Testaments. For example, the Book of Daniel reads: . . . *the Ancient One came; then judgement was given for the holy ones*[25] *of the Most High* . . . (Daniel 7:22). In the New Testament it is reported by Matthew that *many bodies of the saints who had fallen asleep were raised* (Matthew 27:52). On this subject Saint Paul writes: . . . *but you are citizens with the saints and also members of the household of God* (Ephesians 2:19). However, this statement is ambiguous. Does Paul mean the saints who are living or the saints who have passed on? Certainly Paul refers elsewhere to Christian people as saints, for example in the greeting of one of his letters: *To the church of God that is in Corinth, including all the saints throughout Achaia* (2 Corinthians 1:1). However, in his first letter to Thessalonica he writes: *may he so strengthen your hearts in holiness that you may be blameless before our God and Father at the coming of our Lord Jesus with all his saints* (1 Thessalonians 3:13). This surely confirms that the saints who have passed on have a spiritual reality in the eyes of the Church.

Furthermore, given the Christian belief in the resurrec-

---

[25] Translated as "saints" in some versions of the Bible.

tion of the faithful, there seems to be little doubt that there are saints in heaven as well as saints on earth. The question is, however, what does the creed mean? Does the communion of saints, as mentioned in the creed, involve only Christians still living, or does it include those who have passed on? Are angels included? It seems sensible to conclude that all the saints (aspiring holy ones) and heavenly beings are bound together in communion with each other and with God. All are surely in God's care.

One important question is whether, apart from angels and the Holy Spirit, there can be communication between the two realms of earth and heaven. Some Christians, for example, believe that saints can intercede for them and that saints may be venerated (not worshipped). Other Christians maintain that the saints in heaven cannot have any influence on the world. However, most Christian groups do admire outstanding Christians of the past and present. The first Christians, for example, paid homage in a general sense to the Church's martyrs. Some groups took this a stage further and treasured relics of martyrs and celebrated the anniversary days of their martyrdom. Polycarp (*c.* AD 69–155) was venerated in this way by his followers.

On the question of the prayers of the saints, the Book of Revelation mentions these in a heavenly context: . . . *the four living creatures . . . fell before the Lamb, each holding a harp and golden bowls full of incense, which are the prayers of the saints* (Revelation 5:8 and see verse 8:3). It is not clear whether the saints here are those on earth, their prayers rising to heaven, or the saints already in heaven. The parable of the rich man and Lazarus, told by Jesus, assumes that the dead can think of the living (see Luke 16:19–31), but the request of the rich man in Hades for help for his brothers is denied. He then asks if the previously poor man,

Lazarus, now in heaven, may be allowed to warn the brothers of the dire fate facing them. This further request is also denied. However, the story is sometimes used to support the idea that the saints in heaven can indeed intercede for those on earth. Even if this argument is not accepted, it is surely the case that the saints in heaven do have a prayer life. It is also probable that they remember their time on earth and the people they met. It would not be surprising, therefore, if they prayed for the welfare of the people they remembered. Yet, that does not necessarily mean that the prayers of earthly saints for help from heavenly saints are mediated by the Holy Spirit.

Even among Christians who do not believe in veneration of the saints, it is often a practice to name a church after a saint, most frequently after one of the apostles. Some churches wish to show their respect to all the saints, naming their church accordingly as *All Saints' Church*. Some such dedications are given to saints who are little known except as a name, possibly of local importance. The Virgin Mary is considered so important that her name is often linked with that of another saint. For example, a church might be dedicated to Saint Mary and All Saints. The implication of such dedications, though some people might deny this, is that there is a hope for the special care of the patron saint or saints.

There are, of course, many unknown saints, that is good and faithful people who proceed after death to the realm we call heaven. These saints are just as important as the famous saints like Saint Francis and Saint Jerome. Nevertheless it is true that in most cases the famous saints have lived outstanding lives in the service of Christ. In the Roman Catholic Church there is a rigorous examination of the evidence before anyone is declared a saint. In Protestant churches people like Martin Luther, John Wesley and David Livingstone are admired as great Christians, but such churches do not declare particular people to be saints in any special way. When the history of the Church in all its denominations is considered, there is a wonderful "cloud of witnesses"[26] who have served Christ in their own time and in their own way.

The importance of belief in the communion of saints, despite varying views, is that each Christian is part of a community in fellowship with Jesus Christ. The value of this communion is very much emphasised in the sacrament of Holy Communion (the Eucharist) in which groups of Christians are in communion with each other and with God. This is a great inspiration for daily living.

Questions for Discussion

○ *How would you define a saint?*
○ *If you were founding a new organisation to help deprived people, which saint would you choose to be patron?*
○ *Do you think there are any living saints?*

[26] Quoted from Hebrews 12:1.

CHAPTER TWENTY

The Forgiveness of Sins

In their relationships with others, the vast majority of people have experienced some kind of hurt received from someone, or hurt given to someone. It is never easy to forgive and it is often just as difficult to accept forgiveness. Christians are aware that they are also in relationship with God. The same difficulties apply. It is not easy for God to forgive. In fact, one of the main purposes of the Incarnation and the Passion of Christ was to offer divine forgiveness at great cost. Unhappily, it is sometimes not easy for people to accept God's forgiveness because they cannot rid themselves of bitterness and hate. That they are not in the right state of mind to receive forgiveness may be partly because they have not forgiven people who have hurt them. The Lord's prayer makes this clear: *Forgive us our trespasses as we forgive those who trespass against us.* The parable of Jesus about the unforgiving servant illuminates this point. One servant is released from his debt by his master, while at the same time not releasing his fellow servant from his debt. The unforgiving servant is punished. Jesus ends the story with the punch line: *So my heavenly Father will also do to every one of you, if you do not forgive your brother or sister from your heart* (see Matthew 18:23–35). Moreover, our forgiveness should not be abandoned in despair after several attempts at reconciliation. In reply to Peter's question on the number times a person should forgive, Jesus replied: *Not seven times, but I tell you, seventy seven times (*or *seventy times seven)* (Matthew 18:21–22).

Another important condition of the divine forgiveness is the need for true penitence. Those who return to God in penitence, or who turn to God for the first time, will not be refused love, mercy and forgiveness. The parable of the prodigal son illustrates this very well. After leaving home with his share of the family wealth, he wastes his life in riotous living. As the years pass he becomes very unhappy and decides to return home with the intention of saying, *Father, I have sinned against heaven and before you. I am no longer worthy to be called your son . . .* (Luke 15:18–19). The father receives his long lost son back into the family with great joy (see Luke 15:11–32). One of the purposes of Jesus in telling this parable was to explain that penitence by us and the divine forgiveness go hand in hand.

Some inspired writers of the Old Testament explore the idea of forgiveness. In the book of Isaiah, for example, we read: *I have swept away your transgressions like a cloud, and your sins like a mist; return to me, for I have redeemed you* (Isaiah 44:22). Psalm 51 also expresses the idea of God's forgiveness in beautiful words: *The sacrifice acceptable to God is a broken spirit; a broken and contrite heart, O God, you will not despise* (Psalm 51:17). Even more significant as a pre-Christian exploration of God's wish to forgive is one of the beautiful poems about the suffering servant, also in Isaiah: *But he was wounded for our transgressions, crushed for our iniquities; upon him was the punishment that made us whole* (Isaiah 53:5). Many people see this poem (Isaiah 52:13 – 53:12) as a prophecy about the work of Christ in redemption.

Both Old and New Testaments use a variety of words to express the idea of forgiveness. It would be impossible to discuss all of these without undertaking a complicated word study.[27] However, one such word is of great interest, that is, the Hebrew word for *cover* or *atone* (*kāphar*). The idea behind this word is important because the Old Testament concept of atonement became a key concept in the New Testament. In ancient Israel the high priest confessed the sins of the nation on the Day of Atonement, placing his hands on the scapegoat which then supposedly carried away those sins into the wilderness, where it was released (see Leviticus 16). Paul, in particular, takes up this idea and shows its importance in relation to the atoning work of Christ (see, for example, Romans 5:10 and Colossians 1:22). In another place Paul writes: . . . *Christ Jesus, whom God put forward as a sacrifice of atonement by his blood, effective through faith* (Romans 3:24–25). The author of the first letter of John writes: . . . *Jesus Christ the righteous, and he is the atoning sacrifice for our sins, and not for ours only, but also for the sins of the whole world* (1 John 2:1–2).

At the Last Supper Jesus explained that his body and blood were signified by the bread and wine he was sharing with his disciples. This sharing of himself would also take place in the future, whenever the sacrament of communion was celebrated. Paul's account of the Last Supper is probably the earliest recorded in the Bible (see 1 Corinthians 11:23–26). The sacrament, of course, is a memorial of Christ's sacrifice on the cross. The author of the letter to the Hebrews explains clearly the atoning value of Christ's sacrifice on the cross: . . . *he has no need to offer sacrifices day*

---

[27] Some of the words used in English translations include: expiation, reconciliation and justification – all of which would require substantial explanation.

after day (like the Jewish high priest), *first for his own sins, and then for those of the people; this he did once for all when he offered himself* (Hebrews 7:27). Christ, in fact, presides over the sacrament of communion as our great high priest in heaven, but is also the one who offers himself as the sacrifice.

Another important sacrament of the Church, baptism, is also to do with forgiveness. This association is exemplified in Peter's exhortation to some early converts to the faith; *He said to them, "Repent, and be baptized every one of you in the name of Jesus Christ so that your sins may be forgiven . . . "* (Acts 2:38). Whenever adults are baptized today, it is assumed that they have repented of any sins they have committed, and that they are forgiven. (The case of infant baptisms is rather different and varying views are expressed by different denominations.) Baptism, of course, is the rite of entry into the Church.

A further important idea related to forgiveness is to do with the Exodus and redemption, and associated with these the sacrifice of the Passover lamb. In Jewish practice the Passover came to signify spiritual redemption for all Jewish people. It is significant that in John's Gospel John the Baptist is reported as saying of Jesus: *Here is the Lamb of God who takes away the sin of the world* (John 1:29). On this subject Paul writes: *For our paschal lamb, Christ, has been sacrificed* (1 Corinthians 5:7). In another place Paul also writes: *. . . his beloved Son, in whom we have redemption, the forgiveness of sins* (Colossians 1:13–14). In redemption there is included the idea of paying for some one to be released, for example, a slave. With reference to Christ, this implies that he has paid for our sins.

Guilt on the one hand, and unwillingness to forgive on the other hand, are very destructive forces within us. The alternatives, that is, generosity in forgiveness and a repentant acceptance of the divine forgiveness, lead to peace of mind and a close relationship with Christ. Follow the teaching of Christ, forgive and be forgiven, and: *Rejoice in the Lord always . . . and the peace of God which surpasses all understanding, will guard your hearts and minds in Christ Jesus* (Philippians 4:4–7). God cares for us and loves us. Do we love him, and do we love and care for our neighbour? Love, mercy and forgiveness go hand in hand.

Questions for Discussion

○ *What advice would you give to quarrelling friends?*
○ *Should judges in law courts have elements of forgiveness in their judgements?*
○ *In what senses could Jesus be seen as (a) a scapegoat, (b) a Passover lamb*

⊰ CHAPTER TWENTY-ONE ⊱

The Resurrection of the Body

The resurrection of Jesus has been discussed in an earlier chapter. This item of the creed is about us. For Christians, and perhaps for everyone, a resurrection of some sort follows our departure from this life. To be a Christian is to believe in such a resurrection. However, the nature of our resurrection is mysterious. It may not be like waking up in the morning after a night's sleep. Furthermore, the nature of the resurrection body is not known to us except in very general terms. Saint Paul believes our heavenly bodies will be different from our earthly bodies. He writes: *It is sown a physical body, it is raised a spiritual body* (1 Corinthians 15:44). He also writes: *Just as we have borne the image of the man of dust, we will also bear the image of the man of heaven* (1 Corinthians 15:49). In this passage Paul is making the point that there definitely is a resurrection of the body, but that our new bodies will not be the same as our existing bodies. However, he does not give a detailed description of the spiritual body, presumably because, though his conviction was strong, his knowledge, like ours, was limited.

There are many statements in the New Testament about the resurrection of Christians. Jesus, of course, promises eternal life to believers: *Very truly, I tell you, anyone who hears my word and believes him who sent me has eternal life, and does not come under judgement, but has passed from death to life* (John 5:24). However, even Jesus does not give details about what our resurrection bodies will be like. Paul's writings are very rich in repeating the promise of another life after this one. To take but one example, he writes: *For since we believe that Jesus died and rose again, even so, through Jesus, God will bring with him those who have died* (1 Thessalonians 4:14). Peter also promises a re-birth and writes: *By his great mercy he has given us a new birth into a living hope through the resurrection of Jesus Christ from the dead, and into an inheritance . . . kept in heaven for you* (1 Peter 1:3–4). That strange book of poetic prophecy, Revelation, provides a clear vision of the after life: *And I saw the dead, great and small, standing before the throne, and books were opened* (Revelation 20:12). The books mentioned supposedly contained records of the actions of everyone who had lived upon earth.

An interesting question is whether the appearances of the risen Jesus throw any light on the nature of our resurrection bodies. Jesus' body was substantial enough to be touched by Thomas (John 20:27) and Jesus also ate some food (Luke 24:42–43). Although not immediately recognisable at some times, in most of the appearances people could see who he was. This evidence seems to suggest that our risen bodies may have substance and that we may also be recognisable in the next life to those who have known us. Of course, our conclusions cannot be too definite here because the resurrection of Jesus was unique.

Another interesting question is, if our earthly bodies return to dust, how can they be re-made? The survival of consciousness is a related question. In either case it could be argued that God holds us in being in the here and now, and that he can remember our individual creation formula and re-create it. A modern parable may illustrate this idea.

If God is compared to a master computer and each of us is compared to a floppy disk written by the computer, then if the floppy disk is lost or destroyed, all the data is still on the master disk and another floppy disk can be made. Furthermore, additions and alterations may be made to the new floppy disk, but it still contains essentially the same documents, though edited. In a similar way, God may preserve us and re-make us – possibly with amendments (improvements).

It is inevitable that supposition and speculation must be part of our search to try to discover what our new heavenly bodies might be like. However, reason and logic may be of some help. For example, the bodies we rent in this life are magnificent creations and the experiences we have with the help of those bodies and their senses can often be wonderful, though sometimes unhappy. Is it likely that our resurrection bodies will be less wonderful than those we have at the moment? Is it not more likely that our new bodies and our new experiences will be even more wonderful? There may indeed be parameters of the mind and body which are unimaginable. We may have powers of perception and action which are much more varied than our present ones.

Some people think of a life after death with dimensions of peace and stillness, a life without action, so to speak. To others, such a life would seem infinitely boring. What about all the creative activities we can be involved in here, art, literature, science, music, and so on? It makes more sense to think of a continuation of development in such spheres in the next life, rather than the loss of selfhood in the infinite. It is much more likely, surely, that the next life will be full of exciting experiences. These will no doubt include an even richer relationship with God than we have now. Saint

Paul expressed his future hope very well when he wrote that he would much rather be with Christ in heaven, than counting the years in this world (Philippians 1:23).

Questions for Discussion

○ *What is the soul?*
○ *What is the difference between the mind and the brain?*
○ *Are so called out of body experiences convincing?*

CHAPTER TWENTY-TWO

Life Everlasting

As already pointed out, the future life is a mystery. On the face of it, however, the time factor would seem to be a simple matter. Does life everlasting mean exactly what it says: life in heaven goes on for ever? Some people argue that this is the case. On the other hand, some argue that eternity is timeless, which is a concept very difficult for us to understand. After all, we live in a world where time is a basic part of our lives. Time does not stand still. Leaving that problem aside for the moment, what does the Bible tell us about eternal life?

Jesus himself says that people who follow him will receive eternal life in the age to come (Mark 10:30). However, this does not tell us much about what eternity might be like. The translation of the Greek word "eternal" is virtually the same as the word translated "age to come" (adjective and noun from same root). These words (which are the most important ones on this subject) are both frequently used throughout the New Testament. The English word *aeon* is derived from the Greek words used and has been adapted by astronomers to indicate a thousand million years. However the basic meaning of *aeon* is the same as the primary meaning of the Greek noun i.e. an age. This can mean endless time of the past or of the future

– which, of course, does not solve the problem of what eternal life involves.

Paul contrasts the present age with the age to come, as in fact Jesus also does (see Ephesians 1:21 and Matthew 12:32). The idea that this present world is not the real world is implied in a number of texts. For example, Paul writes: *But our citizenship is in heaven, and it is from there that we are expecting a Saviour* (Philippians 3:20). At the same time, there is a sense in which God's kingdom is already here. Jesus himself said: *For, in fact, the kingdom of God is among (or within) you* (Luke 17:21). God's kingdom, of course, must be the dimension in which people experience eternal life. Many of the parables of Jesus are about the kingdom of heaven or the kingdom of God. They are mainly about who can or cannot enter the kingdom (e.g. the ten virgins, Matthew 25:1–13). However, the metaphor of the wedding feast is used in this parable (v. 10). Further, the kingdom is compared to a king's wedding feast. Those originally invited refuse the invitation, so all and sundry are invited (see Matthew 22:1–14). The idea of a special feast in heaven is an aspect of visions of the end time (see Isaiah 25:6–10; Revelation 19:9). These are beautiful metaphors which may echo eucharistic practice, but they do not satisfy our curiosity about the nature of eternal life.

One of the key texts about eternal life is in John's Gospel: *For God so loved the world that he gave his only Son , so that everyone who believes in him may not perish but may have eternal life* (John 3:16). For us to obtain eternal life is God's promise and is one of the main purposes of the Incarnation. Jesus explains to a rich man how to obtain eternal life, that is by keeping God's laws. However, the rich man is unwilling to give up his wealth and thus falls short (Mark 10:17–22). Yet we all fall short, so we must all rely upon

God's grace. As Saint Paul writes (contrasting grace with the dominion of sin): . . . *so that grace might also exercise dominion through justification leading to eternal life through Jesus Christ our Lord* (Romans 5:21).

Jesus several times makes specific promises that eternal life is our destiny. For example, when he announces to Martha that he is the resurrection and the life, he adds: . . . *everyone who lives and believes in me will never die* (John 11:26). This implies that faith is important as preparing us to receive God's grace. Jesus also says: *Very truly I tell you, anyone who hears my word and believes him who sent me has eternal life* . . . (John 5:24 and see 6:40). Eternal life is, in fact, a gift of Christ to the faithful (see John 10:28).

The above paragraphs barely skim the surface of a very complicated subject. Yet, even if all the references in the Bible to eternal life were fully explored, we should not be much the wiser about what kind of life it is. In the previous chapter there was some discussion of the nature of the resurrection body and it was concluded that the next life may well be much more exciting and interesting than this one. At the very least, we can say that we shall be more deeply immersed in God's love than we are in the here and now.

Returning to the question of whether or not there is time in heaven as we understand it, our knowledge again is limited. If departed souls have consciousness along with bodies of some kind, and if there are events of any kind, then it would be reasonable to suppose that time must exist there in some form. However, there may be dimensions in heaven which we cannot even imagine because we are restricted by the parameters of this world, given to us by God. Another important point is that if this world is a preparation for the next world, it would seem likely that there will be some similarities between the two realms.

The most vital factor that has emerged in the above discussion is that Christ *promises* us eternal life. That promise gives us something more than a future hope: it give us a real anticipation of a wonderful experience beyond the grave.

Questions for Discussion

○ *Would living for ever be boring?*
○ *In what ways could we be involved in eternal life in the here and now?*
○ *Is re-incarnation compatible with Christian belief?*

Other Activities

The activities set out below, on a chapter by chapter basis, are suitable for group work. Some of the suggestions are particularly phrased for use with children.

ONE

Make a list of names or titles for God used in the Bible.
Try to describe God using only ten words

TWO

Make a list of biblical texts, hymns, poems or other sources which help you to understand the almighty power of God.

On a large sheet of card write at the top: *Father we ask you*. Each person write a short request and stick it to the card

THREE

List the things in life you are thankful for.

Read the account of creation in Genesis, listing the things made on each day. What would you include if you were writing a poem about creation?

FOUR

List the ways in which the Church can assist the saving work of Christ.

Each person identify his or her favourite parable. Give your reason for your choice.

FIVE

List the ways in which, according to the Gospels, Jesus served other people.

Draw up a plan for encouraging the Church to become more of a family of God.

SIX

Each person write a short prayer ending with the words: *through Jesus Christ our Lord.*

Dramatise the experiences of Thomas (John 20:19–29) and Mary Magdalene (John 20:11–18).

SEVEN

Look at the list of Jesus' ancestors in Matthew (1:1–17) and Luke (3:23–38). Identify the differences.

Read Psalm 2. In what ways could this psalm be seen as a prophesy about Jesus?

EIGHT

Make a list of organisations which are devoted to Mary.

Read the Magnificat (Luke 1:46–55). Now read 1 Samuel 2:1–10). What similarities do you notice between the two passages?

NINE

Compose a prayer for prisoners unjustly held in custody.

Produce a short play portraying the judgement before Pilate.

TEN

Design a cross or crucifix. Explain your use of symbolism.

Read aloud the seven sayings from the cross, with pauses for prayer.

ELEVEN

Write a prayer for the departed and another one for those who are in mourning.

Write an obituary of Jesus for a national newspaper.

TWELVE

Make a list of symbols used in the Bible to describe hell.

Describe what you think hell might be like.

THIRTEEN

Make a list of parables in nature which may prefigure the resurrection e.g. dawn.

Dramatise the appearance of Jesus by the lakeside (John 21).

FOURTEEN

Draw a ladder outline on a large sheet of card. Each person suggest the name of a saint to write on a rung of the ladder. Explain reasons for your choice.

Make a list of experiences you hope to have in heaven.

FIFTEEN

Make a list of words which might be used to describe God's glory.

Using a concordance, find texts in the New Testament which mention Christ as being at God's right hand.

SIXTEEN

Read the ten commandments and Jesus' summary of the law (Exodus 20:1–17 and Matthew 22:37–40). Are these sets of laws in any ways similar? Now read Matthew 19:18–19 and Matthew 5:21–48. What do you conclude about Jesus' view of Old Testament laws?

Act out the parable of the Wicked Tenants (Matthew 21:33–41).

SEVENTEEN

Read Acts 2:5–13. How would you explain the description of people speaking many languages?

Using a concordance, identify texts in Acts of the Apostles which mention the work of the Holy Spirit.

EIGHTEEN

Identify three holy people from the past or the present day.

Why are they holy?

Each member of the group describe any trip made to a holy place.

NINETEEN

Identify the saints who are patrons of churches in your area. Find out some background about one or more of these saints.

Choose a saint who was venerated in medieval times (before the Reformation). Research his or her life story.

TWENTY

Dramatise the story of the Prodigal Son (Luke 15:11–32).
Read Psalm 51. Then share a short period of silent prayer.

TWENTY-ONE

List the characteristics of a heavenly body you would like to have.

Read Ezekiel 37:1–10. Try to express the spirit of this passage in some creative way.

TWENTY-TWO

Spend five minutes in describing how you would like to spend eternity. Share some or all of your thoughts.

Can you think of examples of God's grace working in and through people?